A COMIC STRIP YOU NEVER KNEW YOU LOVED

BY: DAVE JOHNSON

“DEAD AIR” AND “DOG COMPLEX” ARE PROPERTY OF DAVE JOHNSON

If Dave were smart, he probably would have had a Lawyer, or at very least someone with a brain write this page. As it turns out, he's not too bright, and so what you are reading are simply words that have little to no meaning.

All this being said, please don't reprint the contents of this book or try to profit from it in any way, unless given permission by Dave Johnson or someone he thinks is neat.

ISBN 978-1-257-83168-5

The strips contained in this book were produced between 5/11/2003 and 6/10/2011.

FOR TESSA, SEBASTIAN, AND LILY.

A SPECIAL THANKS TO MY SID, P.J.

FOREWORD

Whether you know it or not, you are now holding one of the greatest undiscovered treasures in the history of comic stripdom. Don't even allow yourself for even a second to think I am exaggerating. I'll explain.

I've been a personal friend and creative collaborator of Dave Johnson for over a decade. I watched Dog Complex begin as a hobby strip and steadily evolve into a strip that was acclaimed by industry insiders and eventually was sought after as a paid gig. Dog Complex became one of the rising stars of new comic strips.

I struggled through my youth with a reading disability that nearly vanquished my desire to read. Only the comic strip rescued me from illiteracy. The established greats like Schultz, Breathed, and Watterson kept me laughing and, perhaps more importantly, kept me turning the page. With that level of appreciation for the well-crafted comic strip, I can say without reservation that Dog Complex remains among my favorites. Personally being so close to Dog Complex from the beginning was a daily joy in my life.

The world deserved to see Dog Complex in full color every Sunday morning wrapped around coupons for microwavable dinners and underwear ads from local department stores, but it never happened. There are more cruel events in life for sure, but a minor injustice all the same.

I hope as you turn the page and dive into this, the first volume, that you too embrace Dale and Sid and the gang like I did. After all, your literacy may depend on it.

-Tracy Green
Parts Unknown - June, 2011

CHAPTER 1: RADIO STATIONS AND ROOKIES

Before you read any further, do me a favor and turn to any page between around 75-100.

I just want you to know that things will get better.

In the early days of this strip, my drawings were ugly at best, and I rarely had any sense of direction. Around the halfway mark of this book I think you'll see things build momentum, and by the end I was starting to understand the characters and really develop a feel for how to make a decent comic strip.

In those early days, the strip was called "Dead Air," and it centered on Dale working at the radio station. What I didn't anticipate is that drawing a comic strip at a radio station can get pretty old pretty quickly, because it's a person and a microphone. It's hard to show facial expressions on a microphone and as a result, the drawings got old quickly. So I gave Dale a dog, Sid, to talk to when he got home from work. Then Sid just sort of took over the whole show, eventually resulting in the name change to "Dog Complex." Dale still gives me a hard time about that to this day.

Don't feel cheated by what you hold though, as I firmly stand by the writing throughout this book, even in the early days. Sure a few of the jokes were wild throws that came nowhere near home plate, but even then they entertained, even if it was in a "train wreck" sort of way. So even though the character designs are all over the board (just compare the first and last pages of this collection to see), I hope you'll still get a great deal of enjoyment out of the gags.

Think of this first chapter like the origin of a super hero, only with a lot less "super," and almost zero "hero."

WELCOME TO BURGER DOME! CAN I INTEREST YOU IN OUR NEW LOW-FAT, LOW-CARB, LOW-SELF ESTEEM HAMBURGER?
THAT'S A PICKLE.
CHILE

ACTUALLY, IT'S A FLAME-BROILED PICKLE, COOKED JUST THE WAY YOU LIKE IT. IT'S QUITE TASTY.
FINE, GIVE ME TWO WITH AN ULTRA-BIG COKE.

WE HAVE TEA.
FINE. TWO PICKLES, A TEA AND AN ORDER OF FRIES, AND I'D LIKE TO MONDO-SIZE THEM.

WE HAVE CELERY, AND WE ONLY CARRY SMALL NOW.
CAN'T A MAN BLOCK HIS ARTERIES ANYMORE?!?

The one that started it all. I remember thinking, "Wow... this might be something special!" It wasn't.

BURGER DOME IS GOING ALL HEALTHY TO TRY AND KEEP OUR BUTTS OUT OF BANKRUPTCY.
SO YOU MEAN TO TELL ME THAT ALL MY OLD FAVORITES HAVE BEEN REPLACED?
CHILE
TRY IT!

CHICKEN NUGGETS?
YEP.
BOILED CHICKEN BITS.
FRENCH FRIES?
PATRIOT CELERY.
APPLE PIE?
TURNIP PUDDING.

SO I CAN'T GET ONE THING FROM YOUR MENU ANYMORE THAT IS BAD FOR ME?
SMILE DAMN YOU

I THINK WE HAVE SOME 2 MONTH OLD GREASE ON ONE OF THE OLD FRYERS IN THE BACK. WOULD YOU LIKE ME TO SMEAR YOUR PATRIOT CELERY IN IT?
GOD BLESS YOU MY CHILD.
TRY IT!

WHAT HAPPENED TO ALL OF THE BENCHES?
HAVEN'T YOU HEARD, SIR? BURGER DOME HAS GONE THROUGH A FACELIFT TO MAKE US MORE APPEALING TO CONSUMERS.
TEA
CELERY

WE HAVE REMODELED EACH ONE AFTER THE PROMINENT THEME OF EACH SPECIFIC TOWN.
TED

BUT THIS TOWN HAS NO THEME.
EXACTLY! YOUR TOWN'S THEME IS NOTHING, SO WE TOOK OUT ALL OF THE BENCHES AND TABLES.
TEA
CELERY

MARKETING GENIUS.
OOOH... I'D BETTER GO USE THE JOHN. THEY'RE HERE FOR THE TOILETS.
TEA

THIS IS ALL SO LAME!! NEXT YOU'RE GOING TO TELL ME THAT YOU'VE TAKEN THE TOYS OUT OF YOUR KIDS MEALS!
NOT EXACTLY, SIR, BUT WE HAVE REPLACED THEM.
EAT THIS... OR DIE

REPLACED THEM?
OUR STUDIES HAVE SHOWN THAT KIDS ARE LESS LIKE TO INFLICT SERIOUS BODILY INJURY ON THEMSELVES OR OTHER CHILDREN WITH OUR NEW TOYS.
BURGER DOME FUN MEAL

NEW TOYS?
CHECK IT OUT...

IT'S A HEAD OF LETTUCE.
NOT IN THE VAST MIND OF A CHILD!

Dale spent most of the early strips with his mouth WIDE open. A few months in, an Editor at Universal Press Syndicate pointed this out, and I curbed it from that point on.

SOMEWHERE IN THE NORTHWEST
SO WE'VE SWITCHED TO ALL TALK. MAN THIS IS GOING TO BE TOUGH.
WHNW
I MEAN, TALKING FOR 4 HOURS STRAIGHT IS A LOT DIFFERENT THAN GIVING THE CURRENT TIME AND PLAYING A SONG OR TWO.
I'LL JUST LEAVE IT UP TO MY CALLERS. THEY WILL BE THE LEADER AND I SHALL FOLLOW WHEREVER THEIR CONVERSATIONS TAKE US. HERE GOES NOTHING...
WELCOME BACK TO DALEY DOSE, I'M DALE. CALLER, YOU'RE ON THE AIR!
I'D LIKE TO REQUEST SOME PETER CETERA.
There is a long story behind the radio station call letters, "WHNW," but for now I'll at least tell you that the "HNW" stood for "Hot N' Wormy."

ANYTHING OFF OF HIS SOLO ALBUMS WILL BE FINE. NONE OF THAT STUFF FROM HIS SELLOUT DAYS IN CHICAGO.
SIR, THIS STATION IS ALL-TALK NOW.
SO NO PETER CETERA?
I'M AFRAID NOT, BUT THIS ISN'T A LOST CAUSE. MAYBE YOU AND I CAN TALK ABOUT SOME DYNAMIC ISSUE OF THE DAY THAT IS REALLY CHAPPING YOUR HIDE. IS THERE A SUBJECT YOU'D LIKE TO DISCUSS?
ON AIR
IS THIS HOWARD STER...
NEXT CALLER!!!
ON AIR

SO YOU'RE SAYING THAT YOU THINK IT IS COMPLETELY OKAY WITH YOU?
I'M SAYING I THINK EVERYTHING WILL BE FINE.
DALE, CAN YOU IMAGINE THE DESTRUCTION THAT IS GOING TO BE LEFT IN THE WAKE OF THIS?
SIR, JUST CALM DOWN.
THIS IS GOING TO CAUSE SUCH PAIN AND ANGUISH.
YOU REALLY THINK SO?
ON AIR
I'VE EVEN STOCKED ENOUGH RATIONS FOR 6 MONTHS.
WE ARE STILL TALKING ABOUT WHOOPI GOLDBERG GETTING HER OWN SITCOM, AREN'T WE?
WE'RE ALL DOOMED! KIDS, DOWN TO THE CELLAR!
Long before Whoopi was a member of "The View," she had her own sitcom. I don't think it even lasted a single season.

NOT BAD FOR A FIRST SHOW.
THANKS. IT IS GOING TO TAKE ME SOME TIME TO GET USED TO THIS ALL-TALK FORMAT, BUT I THINK I'M GOING TO LIKE IT.
YEAH, BUT DON'T YOU MISS THE PURE RAW ENERGY OF ROCK AND ROLL RIPPING THROUGH YOUR EARS, AND THE POWER THAT COMES FROM KNOWING THAT ALL OF THOSE KIDS WERE HANGING ON YOUR EVERY WORD?
ROUGH HOUSE
DANNY, WE AVERAGED 12 LISTENERS PER HOUR, AND THE CLOSEST THING TO ROCK WE PLAYED WAS WHAM.
YEAH, THOSE WERE THE DAYS.
Danny's shirts almost always carried the name of an obscure 80s Hair Metal band. This shirt was no exception.

YOU WANNA GO GRAB A DRINK?
SURE, MAYBE THAT SAME BARTENDER WILL BE WORKING, SHE WAS A FOX, AND I THINK SHE LIKED ME.
WHAT?
HIS NAME WAS AL, AND THE AMOUNT OF HAIR ON HIS BACK WAS THE ONLY THING HE HAD IN COMMON WITH A FOX.
YEAH, I THINK I'LL STICK TO MILK TONIGHT.

To keep the final retail price down, I had to go with black and white on this book. It's a shame, because my Photoshop skills were AMAZING back then.

GAME OF DARTS?
YOU KNOW I DON'T PLAY WITH YOU ANYMORE.
C'MON, THAT WAS ONE TIME.
IF YOU START IN ABOUT THIS AGAIN, I'M LEAVING.
SERIOUSLY, IT WAS NOT A BIG DEAL. COULD WE PLEASE BE ADULTS ABOUT THIS AND PUT ONE LITTLE ACCIDENT FIRMLY IN THE PAST, WHERE IT BELONGS?
DANNY, THE DOCTOR SAID ONE INCH TO THE LEFT AND I WOULD HAVE NEVER BEEN ABLE TO HAVE CHILDREN.
WELL, I CAN SEE YOU'RE JUST NOT GOING TO LET THIS GO!!

Another Hair Metal band on Danny's shirt. This time it's Nitro, who had a singer that could shatter glass with his voice, and a guitar player who later threatened to sue me. True story.

WELCOME HOME. HOW DID THE ALL-TALK THING GO AT THE STATION?
WELL, I DIDN'T MAKE A FOOL OF MYSELF.
NOBODY THOUGHT THAT YOU WOULD, DALE. YOU'RE A BRIGHT MAN, AND YOU RELATE WELL TO PEOPLE. I THINK IT WILL BE A GOOD FIT FOR YOU.
SO THAT'S IT, ISN'T IT?
THAT'S WHAT?
WE'VE COMMITTED TO TALKING ANIMALS.
YEAH, AND NOW THAT WE HAVE, I SHOULD PROBABLY TELL YOU THAT I POOPED IN YOUR SLIPPER AGAIN.

Sid shows up for the first time, and with him comes the first of many poop and pee jokes.

WELL IF THIS STRIP IS GOING TO HAVE TALKING ANIMALS, THEN YOU'RE IT. I DON'T WANT TALKING RACCOONS OR TALKING PIGMY GOATS OR SOMETHING.
ACTUALLY DALE, I WAS WONDERING IF WE COULD HAVE ONE OTHER ANIMAL, OF THE SPEAKING PERSUASION, JOIN US.
A FRIEND?
YEAH, HE'S BEEN OUT OF WORK FOR A WHILE, AND HE COULD USE A HAND. PLUS I THINK OUR READERS WOULD REALLY RELATE TO HIM.
NO WAY! I'M NOT HAVING SOME FREELOADER STAYING WITH US, JUST TO BOOST THE RATINGS OF THE STRIP.
HE SAID, "NO WAY."
WELL I, FOR ONE, NEVER SAW THIS COMING.

Apologies to Mr. Breathed.

SID, DID YOU PIDDLE ON THE FLOOR AGAIN?
HEY, YOU NEED TO TAKE ME FOR A WALK MORE OFTEN.
I TOOK YOU OUT 10 MINUTES AGO.
DALE, I HAVE A SHY BLADDER, SO I CAN'T GO WITH YOU WATCHING. PLUS, HOW WOULD YOU LIKE IT IF YOU HAD TO HAVE THE BATHROOM DOOR OPENED FOR YOU EVERY TIME YOU HAD TO "DO YOUR THING" AND THEN I STOOD OVER YOU WITH A ROPE TIED TO YOUR NECK AND WATCHED YOU GO?
FIRST OF ALL, DON'T EVER USE THE TERM "DO YOUR THING," AGAIN. SECOND, MAYBE YOU SHOULD HAVE ASKED FOR OPPOSABLE THUMBS INSTEAD OF THE ABILITY TO SPEAK.
YEAH, AND MAYBE YOU SHOULD HAVE ASKED FOR A STEAM CLEANER FOR YOUR BIRTHDAY.

Let's start a drinking game where you have to drink (milk for you kids) each time a pee joke is made from this point on. My bet is that you won't make it halfway through the book before passing out.

I'M LATE FOR WORK. HAVE YOU SEEN MY KEYS?
DID YOU CHECKED THE KEY RACK?
NO, IN LOOKING FOR MY KEYS, THE THOUGHT NEVER ONCE CROSSED MY MIND TO CHECK THE ONE RACK IN OUR HOUSE WITH THE VERY THING I AM LOOKING FOR CONTAINED WITHIN ITS NAME.
WELL CHECK THERE FIRST THEN, AND IF YOU DON'T FIND THEM, YOU MAY WANT TO TRY LOOKING IN THE IGNITION OF THE CAR.

YOU'RE LATE.
I KNOW, I COULDN'T FIND MY CAR KEYS.

WELL, I FIGURED THAT YOU MIGHT BE IN A HURRY WHEN YOU GOT IN, SO I WROTE UP SOME TOPICS FOR YOU TO DISCUSS ON TODAY'S SHOW.

SALINE OR SILICONE, WHICH ONE IS MORE "BOOBALICIOUS"?
YEAH, THAT ONE SHOULD GET THE PHONES GOING.

The strip was set in the Pacific Northwest, and the call letters for the station were "WHNW." That is until my good friend, Bob, informed me that stations west of the Mississippi always start with a K.

DANNY, I AM NOT GOING TO DO A SHOW ABOUT BREAST IMPLANTS, OR ANY OF THESE OTHER RIDICULOUS TOPICS THAT YOU'VE SUGGESTED.

YOU NEVER LET ME WRITE FOR THE SHOW. HOW DO YOU EXPECT ME TO GET BETTER IF YOU DON'T LET ME TRY OUT TOPICS AND SEE WHICH ONES WORK? WHY DO I EVEN BOTHER WORKING HERE?

YOU KNOW? YOU'RE RIGHT. I SHOULD LET YOU WRITE MORE. HECK THESE AREN'T TOO BAD, I GUESS. OKAY, PICK A TOPIC FROM THE LIST AND I'LL TALK ABOUT IT TODAY, I PROMISE.
NUMBER SEVEN.

"LIKE TWO CHUNKS OF WET MEAT IN A GYM SOCK: A BEGINNER'S GUIDE TO SUMMERTIME SEX."
SEE, I DREW SOME STICK FIGURES.

Another Hair Band on Danny's shirt. This time it's Faster Pussycat, who had a modest hit with a song called, "House of Pain."

FORGET THE BOOB-TALK BUDDY, I'VE GOT A GUEST BOOKED FOR YOU TODAY.
REALLY? WHO IS IT?

I WANT TO KEEP IT A SURPRISE.
DANNY, YOU KNOW I DON'T DO WELL WITH SURPRISES, SO JUST TELL ME WHO YOU BOOKED.

NOPE, BUT I'LL GIVE YOU A HINT: THE GUEST IS A MALE, HE IS FAMOUS, HE LIVES UNDERGROUND, HAS TONS OF CASH, AND IS HATED BY ALMOST EVERY HUMAN IN THE FREE WORLD.

HOLY CRAP, I'M GOING TO GET TO INTERVIEW BILL GATES.

This strip was obviously written long before I became gainfully employed under Mr. Gates...

YOU HAVE TO TELL ME WHO IT IS.
NO CAN DO.

DANNY, WE GO ON IN 20, AND I'D LIKE TO KNOW WHO I'M ABOUT TO INTERVIEW. I HAVE TO KNOW WHAT QUESTIONS TO ASK.
I'VE GOT QUESTIONS WRITTEN FOR YOU.

WELL I'D LIKE SOME BACKGROUND INFO ON HIM, SO THAT I CAN RELATE TO HIM ONCE HE'S ON THE PHONE WITH ME.
TRUST ME, YOU WON'T NEED BACKGROUND INFO WITH THIS GUY.

YOU'RE LOVING THIS, AREN'T YOU?
JUST A LITTLE BIT.

JUST TELL ME!
OKAY! OKAY! I BOOKED YOU AN EXCLUSIVE INTERVIEW WITH SADDAM HUSSEIN! NOW RELAX!

NO YOU DIDN'T.
YES I DID! I SWEAR TO YOU THAT I HAVE HIM SCHEDULED FOR THE NINE O'CLOCK HOUR VIA PHONE!

LIKE THE TIME YOU SWORE AEROSMITH WAS GOING TO BE IN THE STUDIO?
SO THE STEVEN TYLER I CALLED TURNED OUT TO BE A TOW-TRUCK DRIVER FROM OHIO. HOW WAS I TO KNOW?

HE SORT OF LOOKED LIKE HIM THOUGH, DIDN'T HE?
YEAH, RIGHT DOWN TO THE MISSING TOOTH, OVERALLS AND EYE PATCH.

IF YOU'RE NOT LYING THEN TELL ME HOW YOU GOT IN TOUCH WITH THE SADDAM HUSSEIN, LET ALONE GOT HIM TO AGREE TO BE ON THE SHOW.
MY COUSIN IS MARRIED TO A GIRL WHOSE BROTHER IS IN THE ELITE REPUBLICAN GUARD.

AND HE SET THIS WHOLE THING UP?
YEP, I JUST HAD TO MAKE A FEW PHONE CALLS.

YOU'RE SERIOUS? YOU ARE SERIOUS. DANNY DO YOU REALIZE HOW BIG THIS IS?
IT REALLY WAS NO BIG DEAL.

OH MY GOD, DANNY, HOW CAN I EVER THANK YOU?
A SIMPLE "THANK YOU" WILL DO JUST FINE. THAT AND A PLACE FOR 3 OUT OF WORK ELITE REPUBLICAN GUARDS TO SLEEP WHEN THEY MOVE HERE NEXT MONTH.

OH CRAP... THIS IS SO BIG.

I'M GOING TO BE INTERVIEWING SADDAM HUSSEIN. A MAN WHO STRIKES FEAR AND HATRED INTO EVERYONE WHO UTTERS HIS NAME. PEOPLE CURSE HIS VERY NAME!

I WONDER IF THIS IS HOW LETTERMAN FEELS JUST BEFORE HE INTERVIEWS CARROT TOP?

I never realized how much Dale's hair began to look like a newsboy cap.

SADDAM HUSSEIN? THAT IS AMAZING, DALE. I BET YOU'RE REALLY EXCITED.

WELL YES, I'M SURE IT IS A BIG DEAL.

SOMETHING TO LIGHTEN THE MOOD? OH YOU KNOW I'M NOT GOOD WITH TOPICAL HUMOR, DALE, I WOULDN'T KNOW WHAT TO SAY... WAIT I'VE GOT SOMETHING...
BREAD

NO I WILL NOT ASK HIM IF HE NOW REFERS TO IT AS HIS "BUNKER BUSTER."

This one always gives me a chuckle. Sid making a sandwich was also the start of a trend, as by the end of this book, he's eating something in almost every strip.

OKAY DALE, AFTER THE OPENING WE'LL GO STRAIGHT TO SADDAM, ON LINE 3. JUST AN FYI, HE IS IN HIDING, SO HE ISN'T GOING TO WANT TO SAY ANYTHING ABOUT HIS LOCATION.

RIGHT, NO PROBLEM.
WE'RE ON IN 3... 2... 1...

FOLKS, WE'VE GOT AN EXCLUSIVE INTERVIEW FOR YOU TODAY... LIVE FROM PARTS UNKNOWN, THE OUSTED LEADER OF IRAQ, SADDAM HUSSEIN.

...CAN WE ALSO GET A #3, WITH NO PICKLES? SUPER-SIZE THEM WITH... ARE WE ON? OH CRAP AND A HALF!! ABDUL, I TOLD YOU TO WARN ME!

The Saddam Hussein storyline really worked, and brought in a lot of new readers. Plus it was the one and only time I really felt like the radio station premise worked.

SADDAM, WHAT HAS KEPT YOU FROM BEING CAUGHT?
CONSTANT MOVEMENT AND A LOVE FOR SAND DUNES.
KHNW

BUT IT MUST BE HARD TO CONSTANTLY BE ON THE MOVE, ESPECIALLY AFTER THE LIFE YOU HAD PRIOR TO THE WAR.
IT SUCKS THE BIG FAT ONE.

WHAT WOULD YOU SAY SADDAM HUSSEIN'S BIGGEST THREAT IS?
DEFINITELY THE HOLY WAR.

THAT SURPRISES ME...
I MEANT THAT I HAVEN'T BATHED IN WEEKS. I HAVE A JIHAD GOING ON IN MY SHORTS AS WE SPEAK.

SADDAM, WHAT DOES SADDAM THINK ABOUT, WHEN HE'S ALL ALONE IN THE DESERT?
YOU DID IT AGAIN.
NELSON

DID WHAT?
THAT BARBARA WALTERS THING WHERE YOU ASK ME A QUESTION ABOUT MYSELF IN THE THIRD PERSON.

SO?
SO, I THAT IS HER THING, DALE. YOU SHOULD BRANCH OUT AND BE YOUR OWN PERSON.

HEY, SADDAM, HOW ABOUT YOU NOT TELL ME HOW TO RUN A RADIO INTERVIEW, AND I NOT TELL YOU HOW TO LOSE A WAR?
THAT ONE HURT, DALE.

SADDAM, ARE THERE WMDS IN IRAQ?
OH SURE. I MEAN, NOT AS MANY AS SAY MCDONALD'S, BUT WE HAVE THEM.

AND I DON'T SUPPOSE YOU WOULD LIKE TO MENTION WHERE THEY ARE?
I THINK ONE IS ON THE CORNER OF SADDAM ST. AND HUSSEIN AVE. ANOTHER IS LIKE 3 BLOCKS NORTH.

I'M SURPRISED YOU'D GIVE THIS INFORMATION UP.
WHAT DO I CARE IF YOU KNOW WHERE SOME FAST FOOD RESTARAUNTS ARE?

I SAID WMDS, YOU KNOW, WEAPONS OF MASS DESTRUCTION.
A THOUSAND APOLOGIES, I THOUGHT YOU SAID "WENDY'S."

WELL THIS IS A HUGE SURPRISE AND HONOR. I'M BEING TOLD THAT PRESIDENT GEORGE W. BUSH IS JOINING US. MR. PRESIDENT, HOW ARE YOU TODAY?

I'M DOING FINE, DALE.
DO YOU HAVE SOME WORDS FOR SADDAM?
NO TRESSPASSING
ESPECIALLY HILLARY

I CERTAINLY DO. LISTEN HERE, SADDAM, YOU ARE THE LOWEST FORM OF CRUD... YOUR CLOCK IS RUSTY... AND THE CHICKEN IS ABOUT TO LAY THE GOLDEN... UH...GANDER?

ISN'T HE CUTE, DALE?
THAT'S IT. LAURA, FIRE UP THE SUBURBAN WE'RE DRIVING TO IRAQ.

SADAAM, I'D ALSO LIKE TO ADD THAT IT WASN'T VERY FUNNY OF YOU TO LEAVE THAT NOTE BEHIND SAYING THAT THE WMDS WERE IN THAT CAN OF PEANUTS. THE SNAKES ALMOST GAVE ME A HEART ATTACK.

OH, BUSHY, YOU KNOW I KID.
WELL YOU HAD BETTER START TALKING, BUDDY.

FINE... I'LL TELL YOU WHERE EVERYTHING IS.
GOOD.

HEAD TO A TOWN CALLED CLOUD CITY ABOUT 20 MILES NORTH OF BAGHDAD. IT IS THERE THAT YOU WILL MEET UP WITH A MAN BY THE NAME OF LANDO...
HANG ON, I'M WRITING THIS DOWN.

WE'RE OUT OF TIME. I'D LIKE TO THANK THE PRESIDENT FOR JOINING US.
THANK YOU, DALE.

SADDAM, ANY FINAL WORDS?
THE OINTMENT IS IN THE GLOVEBOX RUB IT GENTLY BETWEEN THE TWO CHEEKS.

OH, DEAR LORD... I THINK SADDAM JUST ISSUED SOME KIND OF CRYPTIC MESSAGE...

RELAX, DALE. I WAS SPEAKING TO MY GUARD. DO YOU HAVE ANY IDEA WHAT SAND BUILD-UP IN YOUR SHORTS CAN DO?

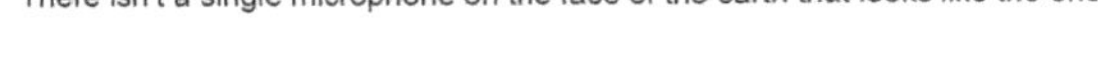
There isn't a single microphone on the face of the earth that looks like the ones I drew.

GREAT INTERVIEW WITH SADDAM... ONE SMALL PROBLEM.
I'M SURE IT ISN'T THAT BIG OF A DEAL.

WELL... OUR COMPUTERS HAVE SOME SORT OF VIRUS. CALLERS HAVE BEEN HEARING STATIC FOR THE LAST HOUR, AND I SORT OF FORGOT TO RECORD THE INTERVIEW.

THUD!

I WAS KIDDING. WE'RE JUST OUT OF T.P. IN THE JOHN AGAIN.
LEAN... CLOSER... I... CAN'T REACH... NECK...

SHOOT! DALE IS GOING TO BE HOME SOON AND I HAVEN'T EVEN STARTED ON HIS CAKE.

MAN I HOPE HE DOESN'T GET HOME EARLY AND RUIN THE SURPRISE.
MILK BONE

SURPRISE!
WHY DOES IT SMELL LIKE BURNT ARMPIT IN HERE?

SID... A CAKE... YOU SHOULDN'T HAVE... REALLY.
NO BIG DEAL. YOU HAD A BIG DAY, SO I WANTED TO DO SOMETHING NICE.

I NEVER KNEW YOU COULD BAKE.
NEITHER DID I, BUT I STARTED READING YOUR COOKBOOKS...

...IT SEEMED REALLY EASY, SO I JUST DECIDED TO WING IT.

WELL THIS IS ALL VERY... SID, THAT LOOKS LIKE AN EYE... IS THAT AN EYE?
HARD TO SAY... EVERYTHING SORT OF LOOKS THE SAME AFTER IT COMES OUT OF YOUR BLENDER.

I CANNOT BELIEVE YOU USED MY BLENDER. THAT IS SO DISGUSTING.
WELL DUH, IT WAS THE ONLY WAY TO GRIND UP THE TURNIPS.

CAKES DON'T HAVE TURNIPS IN THEM.
OH, AND I SUPPOSE THEY DON'T HAVE SQUIRRELS IN THEM EITHER.

AND IF THAT IS THE CASE, TELL ME WHAT THAT RED STUFF IN THE CENTER OF THE ONE IN YOUR COOKBOOK IS?
POIT!

RASPBERRY FILLING.
OH... WELL THEN THAT WOULD EXPLAIN WHY MY SQUIRREL WAS SEEDLESS.

Believe it or not, this strip actually got me my first hate email. The person said it was a cruel joke, and that animal abuse, even on wild animals, was no laughing matter.

HEY FLEMING, YOUR DOG STUNK UP THE ENTIRE FLOOR LAST NIGHT!
1C

GOOD MORNING TO YOU AS WELL, MS. TREADBOTTOM.
IF HE DOES IT AGAIN, I'M STICKING HIM IN MY GARBAGE DISPOSAL.

DO YOU REALLY THINK DR. PHIL WOULD APPROVE OF YOU TALKING LIKE THAT?
WELL NO, I SUPPOSE WOULDN'T.

PHIL WON'T ALWAYS BE THERE FOR YOU, FLEMING! WATCH YOUR BACK!

FROM THE CREATORS OF THE "LION KING," WALT DISNEY PICTURES PROUDLY PRESENTS THE TALE OF A BOY, HIS PUPPY, AND HIS BEST FRIEND...

RIPPED FROM HIS CANCER-STRICKEN PARENTS AND PLACED IN AN ORPHANAGE, "NO MOMMY, I DON'T WANT TO GO, I LOVE YOU!" JIM FINDS HIS ONLY FRIENDS ARE HIS PUPPY AND HIS BEST FRIEND.

BUT WHEN HIS PUPPY IS RUN OVER, "SNAPPER, YOU CAN'T DIE," AND TIKE IS KILLED IN A FIRE, "TIKE, I WILL NEVER FORGET YOU," JIM LEARNS THE TRUE MEANING OF LOVE FROM A BANJO-PLAYING CAT NAMED BUSTER.

"NOW DON'T YOU FRET AND DON'T YOU CRY, CAUSE I'VE GOT A LITTLE TWINKLE IN MY EYE. SO, PUT ON A HAPPY FACE, AND LET'S DANCE AND SING ALL OVER THE PLACE!"
OH COME ON!

At the time of writing this, I had no idea that animation legend, Don Bluth, had once created a short called, "Banjo the Woodpile Cat."

YES! HERE IT IS! THE NEW ONE FROM EDDIE MONEY!

EDDIE MONEY - "LOVE MUFFIN" DOWNLOAD STATUS: 14%

DOWNLOAD CANCELLED DEAR PIRATE SCUM: YOU ARE BEING SUED FOR $150,000 BY THE RIAA FOR ILLEGAL SONG SWAPPING. HAVE A GREAT DAY.

WELL, AT LEAST THIS IS GOING TO MAKE THE PEE ON THE SOFA SEEM RATHER TRIVIAL.

MAN, I AM SO DEAD. THE RIAA IS SUING ME FOR $150,000. THIS IS SO BAD.

OH, YOU KNOW WHAT? THIS IS STUPID. THE RIAA WOULD NEVER SUE SOMEONE LIKE LITTLE OLD ME.

WOULD THEY?

A DORM ROOM, SOMEWHERE IN TEXAS
DON'T MOVE YOU PIECE OF #$*&#!
I WANT THAT COMPUTER CHECKED ASAP! MOVE! MOVE! MOVE!
R.I.A.A. S.W.A.T.
IT WAS ONE DEBBIE GIBSON SONG!

R.I.A.A. S.W.A.T.
SOMETIMES I REALLY AM DUMB. LIKE THE RIAA WOULD REALLY COME AFTER A DOG FOR DOWNLOADING SONGS OFF OF THE NET.

What is that guy next to the truck doing? Who walks like that?

JOHNSON! WHAT'S THE SITUATION?

THE PERP IS 4 FEET TALL, AND DOESN'T APPEAR TO BE DANGEROUS.
THIS PIECE OF DIRT DOWNLOADED PIRATED SONGS. WATCH YOUR STEP.

SIR, I DON'T THINK WE NEED TO BE TOO CONCERNED.
THAT KIND OF TALK IS GOING TO GET ONE OF MY MEN SHOT.

SIR, THE PERP IS AN UNARMED WEENIE DOG THAT DOWNLOADED ONE EDDIE MONEY SONG.
OBVIOUSLY CRAZY FROM THE RABIES.

SID JUST CALLED. HE'S IN JAIL.
IN JAIL?!? FOR WHAT?!?!

ILLEGAL SONG SWAPPING. THE RIAA RAIDED YOUR PLACE.
THE POOR GUY. HE'S SO SMALL.

OH DALE, THEY WOULDN'T PUT HIM IN WITH THE HARDENED CRIMINALS.
I HOPE NOT. YOU KNOW HOW HE LIKES TO TALK.

...BUT DARN IT IF THAT EDDIE MONEY DOESN'T WRITE A CATCHY TUNE. WHAT DID YOU SAY YOU WERE IN FOR AGAIN, MR. SKULL?
STRANGLING FANS OUTSIDE OF AN EDDIE MONEY CONCERT.

PAY THEM THE FINE SO THAT I CAN GET OUT OF HERE.
I DON'T HAVE $150,000.
NO LIPS ON GLASS

NO LIPS ON GLASS

ACTUALLY THE TOTAL COMES TO $150,123.14, ON ACCOUNT OF THE DRY CLEANING.
DRY CLEANING?
NO LIPS ON GLASS

THAT RAID WAS PRETTY FRIGHTENING. YOU KNOW I PEE WHEN I GET FRIGHTENED.
NO LIPS ON GLASS

Pee joke. Everyone drink.

DALE, ON BEHALF OF THE RIAA, I WANT TO APOLOGIZE FOR THE TREATMENT OF YOU AND YOUR GOPHER.
HE'S A DOG.

RIGHT... LISTEN, WE HAD NO IDEA THAT YOU WERE "IN THE BUSINESS."
I'M NOT FOLLOWING...

WHAT SAY WE FORGET THIS WHOLE THING AND YOU PUT THIS LATEST SINGLE FROM CHRISTINA INTO HEAVY ROTATION?
DO YOU REALIZE I WORK FOR A TALK STATION?

HOW CAN THEY PUT ME IN JAIL?
HEY DALE, COME ON OVER. I WANT YOU TO MEET MY POSSE.

No idea why I drew the guy from the R.I.A.A. like Casey Kasem.

GREEN PENITENTIARY
"THE YARD"
...THAT IS LEFTIE, HE RUNS GAMBLING. AND BIG RICK, THE GUY TO TALK TO FOR SMOKES.

SUP RICK! YEAH, I GOT THE SMOKES... THANKS A HEAP!
YOU DON'T SMOKE, AND TAKE OFF THAT SCARF!

WHAT, MY HOMIE BANDANA?
ONLY AN IDIOT WOULD WEAR...
TAP TAP
BEEF

OOPS... ALMOST FORGOT. THIS IS SNAKE. HE MAKES THE BANDANAS.
YOU WAS SAYING?
BEEF

MR. FLEMING, WE HAVE LIQUIDATED YOUR ASSETS TO PAY OFF THE FINES OWED TO THE RIAA. YOU AND YOUR DOG ARE FREE TO GO.
YOU SOLD MY STUFF?!?

BUT I DIDN'T EVEN HAVE CLOSE TO $150,000 WORTH OF STUFF.
HOMIE BANDANA

WE GOT $218 OUT OF WHAT WE SOLD, WE'LL CALL IT EVEN.
GREAT NEWS, DALE! THEY MUST HAVE ONLY SOLD PART OF YOUR STUFF!

OH, WE SOLD IT ALL. JUST ISN'T AS BIG A MARKET FOR FADED UNDERWEAR AND STALE WHEAT THINS AS ONE MIGHT THINK.

SO THE RIAA SOLD EVERYTHING I OWN AND HAD ME THROWN IN PRISON, BECAUSE OF ONE EDDIE MONEY SONG?
IN A NUTSHELL, YES.

DO YOU SLEEP WELL AT NIGHT?
HAVEN'T IN YEARS... ON ACCOUNT OF THE BLOOD LUST.

Early in the strip, I tried to never copy and paste an image. That level of pride quickly fell victim to deadlines.

ARE YOU ANGRY?

I HAVE NO $*#@! IDEA WHO EDDIE MONEY IS, AND I TOLD YOU WHEN I PICKED YOU UP... NO TALKING!

THIS APARTMENT NEEDS A GOOD REDECORATING.
HOW SO?

I'M THINKING WE GO ALL SHABBY CHIC!
SHABBY WHAT?

I SEE LOTS OF LACE AND WHITE, BUT WITH A NICE LIVED-IN LOOK.

THAT'S IT. NO MORE HOME AND GARDEN CHANNEL FOR YOU.
COME LOOK AT THE JOHN... IT JUST SCREAMS FEATHERS AND SILK!

This was the first strip I ever drew 100% in Photoshop. Up until this point, I would draw the strip in pencil, scan it in, and then ink it in PS. I miss my pencils.

DALE, CAN WE GET ANOTHER DOG?

WHY?
WELL, YOU GO OFF TO WORK EACH DAY, AND I'M LEFT HERE ALONE...

I NEED SOMEONE TO TALK TO... SOMEONE TO BOND WITH... SOMEONE TO SHARE STUFF WITH!

SOMEONE TO BLAME WHEN YOU PEE ON THE COUCH?
YOU'RE TOTALLY MISSING MY POINT HERE, DALE!
DAILY COM

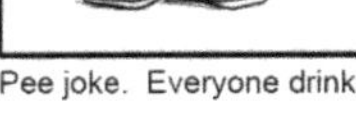
Pee joke. Everyone drink.

WE ARE NOT GETTING ANOTHER DOG.

FINE, THEN FROM THIS MOMENT FORWARD, I NO LONGER SPEAK. WE'LL JUST SEE HOW YOU LIKE LIVING IN SILENCE.

EXACTLY TWELVE SECONDS LATER...
HAVE YOU LOST WEIGHT?

DEAR LORD, SID... WHAT IS THAT?
YOU WON'T BUY ANOTHER DOG, SO I MADE MY OWN.

IS THAT OUR MEATLOAF?
JUST IGNORE HIM, REX.

YOU MOLDED A DOG OUT OF MEATLOAF?
YOU'RE JUST JEALOUS, DALE.

DO YOU HONESTLY THINK THIS IS HELPING YOUR CAUSE?
MORE KETCHUP, OL' BUDDY?

CRAP, EVEN THE MEATLOAF GUILT-TRIP DIDN'T WORK.
JOHNSON

NOW I'M STUCK WITH A GIANT PILE OF MEATLOAF SHAPED LIKE A DOG.

MUNCH
MUNCH

I got a few emails on this one from people telling me how much they enjoyed it, and it was the first time I felt like people were starting to "get" Sid.

WHERE IS YOUR MEATLOAF DOG?
YOU MEAN REX? I ATE HIM.

I'M SORRY TO HEAR THAT.
YEAH, I'M A MOVER AND A SHAKER, HE WAS... WELL... MADE OF MEAT.

YOU GOING TO BE OKAY?
OH, I'LL BE FINE. FRIENDS JUST SORT OF DRIFT APART SOMETIMES.

OR EAT ONE ANOTHER WITH KETCHUP AND A SIDE OF POTATOES.
RIGHT.

SID, YOU REMEMBER MY PRODUCER, DANNY.
HELLO LITTLE GUY!
HELLO HIPPIE!
JOHNSON

SID! THAT IS NOT NICE.
I THOUGHT THAT IS WHAT THEY LIKED BEING CALLED.
NO BIG DEAL, DALE.
JOHNSON

SEE, HE'S NOT OFFENDED.
WELL, I DIDN'T SAY THAT.

GREAT! I'VE OFFENDED THE LONG-HAIR! NO WAY WE'RE GETTING OUT OF HERE WITHOUT A SIT-IN OR SOMETHING!
I'LL BE IN THE CAR.

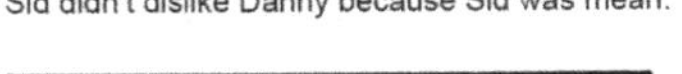

Sid didn't dislike Danny because Sid was mean. Sid disliked Danny because he was Dale's best friend, and didn't want anyone taking his place.

SID, JUST BECAUSE I HAVE LONG HAIR, IT DOESN'T MAKE ME A HIPPIE.
HAVE I OFFENDED YOU?
JOHNSON

NOT REALLY, I MEAN YOU DON'T KNOW ANY BETTER...
WHAT, BECAUSE I'M A DOG?

WELL, NO... I JUST...
AH-HA! IT IS BECAUSE I'M A DOG!

THAT'S RIGHT, HIPPIE BOY, WALK AWAY! JUST DON'T LEAVE ANYTHING LYING AROUND... YOU NEVER KNOW WHEN ONE OF US STUPID DOGS IS GOING TO PEE ON SOMETHING!

Pee joke. Everyone drink.

THINGS AREN'T GOING WELL IN THERE.
DON'T MIND HIM.
BREAD
JOHNSON

I LIKE DOGS, BUT I JUST COULDN'T LIVE WITH ONE.
I KNOW, IT HAS ITS UPS AND DOWNS.
BREAD

AH, DALE... SORRY TO INTERRUPT, BUT SOMEONE PEED ON THE SOFA AGAIN, AND IT WAS NOT ME.
BREAD

THIS WOULD BE ONE OF THOSE "DOWNS," WOULDN'T IT?
YOU HAVE NO IDEA.

Back-to-back pee jokes. Everyone drink, and please try not to barf on this book.

YOU'RE ON THE AIR.
I'VE GOT A TRACTOR I WANT TO TRADE FOR SOME GOATS.

SIR, YOU'RE LOOKING FOR "FARM SWAP," WHICH ISN'T ON THIS STATION.

BUT I WAS TOLD I COULD SWAP MY TRACTOR FOR SOME GOATS.
SORRY, SIR, WE ONLY OFFER ADVICE.

FINE, HOW MANY GOATS DO YOU THINK I CAN GET FOR MY TRACTOR?
JOHNSON

WELL I THINK IT IS MAKING A MOCKERY OF THE SYSTEM.
I'M SURE YOU DO.

HANG ON, DALE, SOMEONE IS AT THE DOOR.

YES? NO, YOU SHOULDN'T BE HERE YET. NO! GET OUT! GET YOUR HANDS OFF OF THAT... NOT UNTIL OCTOBER!

WELL, GOVERNOR DAVIS, I SEE WE'RE OUT OF TIME.
GET YOUR #$@!% HANDS OFF OF ME!

Gray Davis was only the second Governor in the history of the United States to be recalled from office. It turned out to be a "Total Recall," as he was replaced by Arnold Schwarzenegger.

HAPPY LABOR DAY, FOLKS! OF COURSE WE ALL KNOW WHAT HAPPENS ON THIS, MY FAVORITE HOLIDAY!

AS THE CRISP AUTUMN AIR BEGINS TO PUSH AWAY THE SUMMER, THE LABORER SLOWLY PEEKS HIS HEAD OUT OF HIS LOW INCOME HOUSING APARTMENT...

...THEN IF HE SEES HIS TWO WEEKS NOTICE, HE CLIMBS BACK INTO THE WELFARE LINE, AND WE HAVE ANOTHER THREE MONTHS OF LAYOFFS!

UH OH... HERE COMES MR. CEO... YOU KNOW WHAT THAT MEANS...
SID, HAVE YOU SEEN MY SOCKS?

...MADONNA KISSES BRITNEY AND THE NEXT THING YOU KNOW, IT'S SODOM AND GOMORRAH ALL OVER AGAIN.
KHNW

I DON'T THINK IT WAS THAT BIG OF A DEAL, REVEREND. IT WAS JUST ONE KISS.
JUST ONE KISS?

LISTEN DALE, I'VE VIEWED THE TAPE AT LEAST A HUNDRED TIMES. IT WAS MORE THAN JUST ONE KISS. IT WAS SICK AND DISGUSTING.

WELL I CAN SEE HOW A MAN OF YOUR... WAIT... YOU'VE VIEWED IT HOW MANY TIMES?
KNOW THY ENEMY, DALE.

I'm ashamed to admit that, in the original version of this strip, I spelled it "Sadaam and Gamora." I've since taken to spell-checking any word that's more than three letters long.

HEY, SID, I JUST... ARE YOU WEARING A PAIR OF MY BOXERS?
YUP!

YOU DON'T EVEN HAVE LEGS.
SO SHORT LEGS MEAN I CAN'T RELAX?

I GUESS ONLY TALL PEOPLE GET TO WEAR BOXERS WHEN THEY LOUNGE AROUND.

NO, BUT WE DO HAVE THE POWER TO PUT YOUR FOOD UP ON THE COUNTER AND OUT OF YOUR REACH.
COMING OFF!

I'LL GET IT.
RING! RING!
JOHNSON

WELL HELLO MS. TREADBOTTOM. NO, I DON'T KNOW WHO BARFED ON YOUR DOORMAT.

WELL THAT ISN'T VERY NICE. I HOPE YOU DON'T KISS YOUR CHILDREN WITH THAT MOUTH.

IN MY DEFENSE, IT WAS EITHER HER DOORMAT OR OURS.
GOOD BOY.

Again, this is another borderline pee joke. I'll leave it up to you.

DALE? SMALL PROBLEM. I FORGOT WHERE I BURIED MY BONE, SO I HAD TO DIG UP A LARGE PORTION OF THE GRASS OUT FRONT.

JOHNSON

NOW MS. TREADBOTTOM IS STEAMED. SHE SAID IF I HADN'T PUT IT THERE IN THE FIRST PLACE, I WOULDN'T HAVE HAD TO MAKE SUCH A MESS TRYING TO FIND IT AGAIN.

SO GO FIX IT.
WAY AHEAD OF YOU. HOWEVER, I'M GOING TO NEED YOU TO CUT ME A CHECK FOR 87 BILLION DOLLARS FOR THE RECONSTRUCTION EFFORT.

PRESIDENT BUSH MUST NOT ALLOW CHEERIOS AT HIS PRESS CONFERENCES.

I tried to never get too political with the strip, but at times I just couldn't help myself.

OH SID, YOU'VE DONE IT NOW.
JOHNSON

DALE TOLD ME NOT TO PUT SO MUCH STUFF IN THE DISPOSAL AT ONCE AND NOW LOOK...

MAN, I HOPE THAT NEW MAINTENANCE GUY IS AROUND...

?
EXCUSE ME, SIR?
TO BE CONTINUED...

HELLO THERE, ARE YOU OUR NEW MAINTENANCE GUY?
JOHNSON

GET BACK! DON'T YOU THINK I KNOW WHAT YOU ARE?
OH MY LORD!

SIR, I THINK YOU HAVE ME CONFUSED WITH SOMEONE ELSE. I JUST ...

COME ON! WHERE IS THE CAMERA?
SWEET MOTHER OF ALL THAT IS HOLY!

SORRY, LITTLE FELLA. I THOUGHT YOU WERE ONE OF THOSE ***ROBOT-DOGS*** SENT BY THE GOVERNMENT TO SPY ON ME.
YEAH, I GET THAT A LOT.
JOHNSON

YOU SEEM HARMLESS THOUGH. THE NAME'S BOB.
NICE TO MEET YA, BOB! I'M SID.

COURSE YOU LOOK AT ME FUNNY, ***SID***, AND I'LL PUT YOU DOWN LIKE A GAZELLE IN A LION'S DEN.

SO, WAS THERE SOMETHING YOU NEEDED, LITTLE FELLA?
CLEAN SHORTS COME TO MIND.

Bob was based on this crazy Janitor who worked at an apartment complex I lived in. You'd say hi to him, and he'd spend the next 20 minutes telling you how much the Government hated you.

SO WHAT'S IT LIKE BEING A JANITOR, BOB?
JOHNSON

I PREFER CUSTODIAL SUPPORT TECHNICIAN.

YOU WOULDN'T UNDERSTAND, BEING A DOG AND ALL.

I PREFER VERTICALLY CHALLENGED RUMP SNIFFER OF THE FURRY PERSUASION.
TOUCHÉ.

While Bob was based on my old Janitor, he was named after my friend who corrected me on the "KHNW" thing. Naming him after the most insane character in my strip was the least I could do.

SO I LEFT MY WIFE, ON ACCOUNT OF THE MIND CHIP IN HER HEAD, AND MOVED HERE.
HOLD THE PHONE!
JOHNSON

YOU JUST ***UP AND LEFT HER?***
WOULD YOU STAY WITH A MIND-CHIPPED WOMAN?

BOB, ARE YOU ***SURE*** SHE HAD A MIND CHIP IN HER HEAD? YOU COULD HAVE BEEN MISTAKEN.

SHE THOUGHT DAVID HASSELHOFF WAS SEXY.
OH YEAH... ***TOTAL*** MIND CHIP THERE.

WE NEED TO GET RID OF ALL OF OUR ELECTRONIC DEVICES.
ACCORDING TO THE CRAZY JANITOR?

HE'S NOT CRAZY. NOW PUT THIS ON.
WHAT IS THAT?

A TINFOIL BRAIN SHIELD. YOU HAVE TO WEAR IT TO BED AT NIGHT SO THAT THE GOVERNMENT CAN'T SEND YOU SUBLIMINAL THOUGHTS.
JOHNSON

MINE SMELLS LIKE FRIED CHICKEN.
YOU CAN BE SO UNAPPRECIATIVE SOMETIMES!

I CAN TELL WE'RE GOING TO BE GREAT FRIENDS.
ME TOO. IF YOU EVER DOUBLE-CROSS ME, I'LL STRANGLE YOU IN YOUR SLEEP.
I'M FEELING THE LOVE, BOB.

WATCHA' DOING?
HAVING SOME CAKE AND WATCHING "ALL IN THE FAMILY."

THAT SOUNDS LIKE FUN!
NAH. IT'S ONE OF THE EPISODES AFTER EDITH HAD DIED. IT'S JUST NOT AS FUNNY.

I GUESS IT'S TRUE WHAT THEY SAY... YOU CAN'T HAVE YOUR CAKE AND *EDITH* TOO.

THEY CAN'T ALL BE HOMERUNS YOU KNOW!

This one was in reply to all of the, "That last one wasn't very funny," emails I got from time to time.

A DIGITAL CAMERA? COOL!
IT'S GOING TO TOTALLY SIMPLIFY OUR LIVES! I JUST NEED TO CHARGE THE BATTERY, INSERT THE MEMORY STICK, SET THE DATE, AND TAKE PICTURES...

...THEN I PLUG IT INTO OUR COMPUTER, INSTALL THE SOFTWARE, CREATE A DIRECTORY, DOWNLOAD THE IMAGES, SORT THEM INTO SUBDIRECTORIES, AND SAVE EM'...

OKAY, BUT...

...THEN WE INSERT A BLANK CD, INSTALL MORE SOFTWARE, BURN THE PICTURES TO CD, TAKE IT TO TOWN, AND IN 4 TO 6 WEEKS, WE'LL HAVE PHOTOS!
DALE?

WOULD YOU LIKE ME TO GET THE POLAROID AND TAKE A PICTURE OF YOU SMASHING IT?
OH YES, LET'S SIMPLIFY THE #!$@ OUT OF IT!

It's pretty amazing that this strip is 7 years old, and things really haven't gotten any easier.

WHY HELLO LITTLE LADYBUG!

IN THIS CRAZY WORLD, YOU BRING A RAY OF HOPE. HECK, IF SOMETHING AS DELICATE AS YOU CAN SURVIVE, MAYBE WE WILL BE OKAY.

FOR IN A WAY, WE'RE ALL LADYBUGS... SO SMALL AND DELICATE, YET WE SOMEHOW PERSEVERE THROUGH IT ALL.

SID, WHY ARE YOU TALKING TO A WAD OF GUM?
YEAH, I TOTALLY THOUGHT IT WAS A LADYBUG, AND BY THE TIME I REALIZED IT WASN'T, I WAS ON A ROLL.

SID, PLEASE DON'T TELL ME YOU'RE DOWNLOADING MORE PIRATED SONGS.
NAH, I'M VOTING ON BUZZCOMIX!
JOHNSON

DON'T YOU THINK THAT'S KIND OF IMMORAL?
HOW SO?

WELL, WE ARE *IN* THE COMIC. WE SHOULDN'T REALLY BE VOTING FOR OURSELVES.
I'M NOT. I'M VOTING FOR THIS ONE.

WELL I GUESS... WAIT A MINUTE... IS THAT A TALKING ***BLENDER***?
THAT'S BLENDY! HE'S SO CUTE... AND HE SURE KNOWS A LOT ABOUT VIDEOGAMES!

Buzzcomix.net was a website that ranked comics by popularity votes. This strip was intended to get more people to vote for "Dog Complex." Dale's missing chin will be explained a bit later.

CAN I COME WITH YOU TO THE STATION TODAY? I THOUGHT IT MIGHT BE NEAT TO BE YOUR SHADOW.
SURE, BUDDY, LET'S GET YOU FED.

WHO ARE WE INTERVIEWING? SCHWARZENEGGER? LIMBAUGH? I'D LIKE TO ASK HIM SOME QUESTIONS.
ED FROM THE BAIT AND FLY SHOP IN TOWN. HE HAS WORMS FOR 2 DOLLARS.
JOHNSON

NOT EXACTLY BOOB GRABBIN' OR PILL POPPIN', IS IT?
IT SURE ISN'T. NOW EAT YOUR TOAST.

HERE, PUT THIS ON.
YOU ***MUST*** BE JOKING...

OH, HERE WE GO...
NO WAY... YOU AREN'T GOING TO LEAD ME AROUND BY A LEASH ALL DAY, LIKE SOME KIND OF ***ANIMAL***. I HAVE MY PRIDE.

PUT IT ON OR YOU CAN STAY HOME AND WATCH THE "FACTS OF LIFE" MARATHON ON CABLE.
JOHNSON

cafe coffee
BROTHER, I FEEL YOUR PAIN.
OH STOP IT.

WHERE IS MY COFFEE?
DOGS DON'T DRINK COFFEE.
JOHNSON

WELL I AM HURT. FIRST THE LEASH THING, AND NOW I CAN'T EVEN SHARE A COFFEE WITH YOU.

WHERE ARE YOU GOING?
IF YOU'RE GOING TO TREAT ME LIKE A DOG, THEN I'M GOING TO ACT LIKE ONE. I'M GOING TO GET A DRINK.

HOLY CRAP! EVEN THE TOILET WATER IS CAFFEINATED IN THIS PLACE!

WELL THIS IS WHERE I WORK. LET'S HEAD INSIDE AND I'LL INTRODUCE YOU TO THE CREW.
I DON'T WANT TO.
JOHNSON

WHAT? WHY NOT?
I KNOW IT WAS MY IDEA, BUT MIXING YOUR PERSONAL AND PROFESSIONAL LIFE MAY RUIN THE DELICATE BALANCE THAT IS OUR RELATIONSHIP..

KHNW
YOU ARE JUST TOO GOOD A FRIEND TO LET THAT HAPPEN.

DID I MENTION THAT TODAY IS KRISPY KREME WEDNESDAY?
OUT OF MY WAY, DIMPLE CHIN. THE GLAZED ARE BOUND TO GO FIRST.

The KHNW building was modeled after my hometown's radio station, KXLE. I worked at that station for around 4 months.

FOR THE LAST TIME, RUSH LIMBAUGH DOES NOT WORK HERE.
OH I GET IT, KEEP THE BIG STARS BEHIND CLOSED DOORS.
JOHNSON

HE DOESN'T WORK HERE.
OH YEAH? WATCH THIS...

RATTLE! RATTLE! RATTLE!

WHAT ARE YOU DOING?
RATTLING TIC TACS TO TRY AND LURE HIM OUT.
RATTLE RATTLE RATTLE

...AND WHAT I TYPE HERE, DALE CAN READ WHILE HE IS ON THE AIR, LIKE NEWS AND STUFF.
COOL! CAN I TRY IT?

AND A NOTE TO ALL YOU COMMUTERS OUT THERE... 405 IS AN ABSOLUTE MESS, DUE TO A LARGE BLOCKAGE IN MY SHORTS.
JOHNSON

IN RELATED NEWS, THE STATION IS GOING TO BE HIRING A NEW PRODUCER, AND I'VE GOT A FREE DOG TO GIVE AWAY.

I'd like to point out that this strip was released a month before "Bruce Almighty," and a year before "Anchorman," both of which contained similar jokes.

DALE, CAN I COME IN THERE WITH YOU?
SURE, BUT YOU HAVE TO BE QUIET WHILE I'M ON THE AIR.

THIS IS NEAT. I FEEL LIKE A RADIO BIG SHOT.
JUST REMEMBER, NO TALKING.
JOHNSON

AND WE'RE BACK, TALKING WITH STANLEY, WHO FEELS THAT RUSH LIMBAUGH IS ALREADY GETTING AN UNFAIR SHAKE IN THE PRESS.

I'M SORRY TO INTERRUPT, BUT DO YOU EVER WONDER IF YOUR CALLERS ARE WEARING PANTS WHEN THEY CALL IN?

WHY DON'T YOU GO GET ME SOME MORE COFFEE WHILE I FINISH UP THIS LAST SEGMENT?
I'M NOT STUPID.
JOHNSON

YOU'RE JUST SENDING ME OFF TO GET A CUP OF COFFEE BECAUSE YOU THINK I CAN'T KEEP FROM TALKING ON THE AIR!

YOU'RE RIGHT. NOW IT IS THAT, OR YOU CAN WAIT IN THE CAR FOR ME.
LIKE A DOG? FINE, I'LL GET YOUR STUPID COFFEE.

AND WE'RE BACK, TALKING WITH...
HAD TO STOP AT THE JOHN REAL QUICK, CHIEF. YOU TAKE CREAM OR SUGAR IN YOUR GO-GO JUICE?

This one is a borderline pee joke, but I'm worried some of you may already have alcohol posioning, so let's skip it.

DALE, THIS RADIO STATION IS AWESOME! I JUST... SWEET APPLE TURNOVER! WHAT IN THE HECK HAPPENED TO YOUR CHIN?

YEAH... CHARACTER REDESIGN. IT HAPPENS, IT JUST TENDS TO BE A BIT MORE JOLTING IN MID-STORYLINE.
I MEAN, THE CHIN, THE CLEFT, IT... IT'S ALL GONE!

AND THIS CAN HAPPEN AT ANY TIME?
PRETTY MUCH.
JOHNSON

DOES IT HURT?
APPARENTLY NOT AS MUCH AS ONE MIGHT THINK.

Dale's missing chin explained. Sort of.

MAN, THAT WAS GREAT GOING TO WORK WITH YOU TODAY! THANKS, DALE.
SURE THING, BUD.

IT WAS SO NEAT SEEING HOW A RADIO SHOW WORKS.
I'M GLAD YOU LIKED IT.
JOHNSON

THE COOLEST PART WAS WHEN DANNY LET ME RECORD THAT COMMERCIAL FOR YOUR SHOW.
HE WHAT?

WELL, I'M GOING TO HIT THE SACK.
HOLD IT!

HEY EVERYBODY, MY NAME IS SID! MY GOOD BUDDY DALE DOES A MORNING TALK SHOW EVERY MORNING RIGHT HERE ON KHNW!
JOHNSON

I ASK MYSELF, "SID, HOW CAN A GUY WHO HASN'T HAD A GIRLFRIEND IN 2 YEARS, AND HAS TO HAVE HIS PET DOG SHAVE HIS BACK, MAKE SUCH A DARN FINE RADIO HOST?"

I DON'T KNOW, JUST LIKE I DON'T KNOW HOW HE CAN SPEND AN HOUR GOING TO THE BATHROOM. YET HE DOES. SO WON'T YOU TUNE IN? EVERY WEEKDAY MORNING, RIGHT HERE ON KHNW!

WHAT ARE YOU DOING ON THE FLOOR? HAS MY COMMERCIAL BEEN ON YET?

HEY, BOB! I'M THINKING ABOUT TRYING OUT FOR A REALITY SHOW.
REALLY?
JOHNSON

YEAH, THE SHOW IS CALLED "RED HOT ROOMIES" AND IT PUTS 8 PEOPLE TOGETHER IN A HOUSE, TO SEE HOW THEY INTERACT WITH ONE ANOTHER WHILE ON FILE.
ON FILE?

THAT IS WHAT IT SAYS ON THIS ENTRY FORM.
LET ME SEE THAT.

THIS SAYS "WHILE ON *FIRE*."
COOL! I'D WATCH THAT!

I'VE GOT MY APPLICATION FOR THE REALITY SHOW FILLED OUT.
WHERE THEY LIGHT YOU ON FIRE?

NO, I DECIDED AGAINST THAT ONE.
GOOD CALL.

THIS IS JUST A SIMPLE ROOMMATES SHOW... YOU KNOW... WITH THE TOKEN BLACK GUY, THE TOKEN GAY GUY, THE TOKEN HOT CHICK...
JOHNSON

THE TOKEN TALKING DOG WITH BLADDER CONTROL PROBLEMS THAT SCULPTS DOGS OUT OF MEATLOAF, AND HAS AN AFFINITY FOR EDDIE MONEY?
HERE'S TO HOPING.

REC
HOW IN THE HECK DOES DALE OPERATE THIS THING?
JOHNSON

REC
IS IT EVEN ON?

ALRIGHT, WELL I HOPE THIS IS WORKING. MY NAME IS SID, AND THIS IS MY SUBMISSION TAPE FOR "ROOMMATES."
REC

I THINK IT HAS A CERTAIN CHARM.
YEAH, LIKE A ROOT CANAL WITHOUT NOVACAINE.

OH HEY, BOB. I JUST MAILED OFF SID'S APP FOR THAT REALITY SHOW.
TELL HIM GOOD LUCK.

YOU DON'T SOUND ENTHUSED.
I'M JUST NOT A FAN OF THIS REALITY TV STUFF.

SID FILLED OUT A PIECE OF PAPER FOR A SHOT AT FAME AND FORTUNE, BUT WHAT DOES THAT TEACH HIM? WELL, I'LL TELL YOU WHAT... ***NOTHING.***

YOU KNOW, I ACTUALLY KIND OF AGREE WITH YOU. I JUST...
OH CRAP, I GOTTA' RUN. THE LOTTO DRAWING IS IN 5 MINUTES.

AND SO AFTER WEEKS OF WAITING, SID GETS THE PHONE CALL HE'S BEEN WAITING FOR.
RING! RING!

YELLO? **NO WAY!** REALLY? YOU'RE KIDDING, RIGHT?

SURE I CAN BE THERE TODAY! **THANK YOU SO MUCH!** THIS IS THE GREATEST DAY EVER!

WAS THAT THE REALITY SHOW PEOPLE?
BLOCKBUSTER. THE FIRST SEASON DVD OF "WHO'S THE BOSS" CAME OUT A WEEK EARLY!

Sid eventually got much better at drawing. I never did.

THAT WAS THE REALITY SHOW PEOPLE ON THE PHONE... THEY WANT ME ON THE SHOW!
NO WAY!

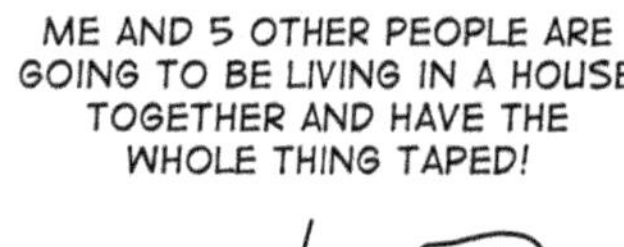
ME AND 5 OTHER PEOPLE ARE GOING TO BE LIVING IN A HOUSE TOGETHER AND HAVE THE WHOLE THING TAPED!

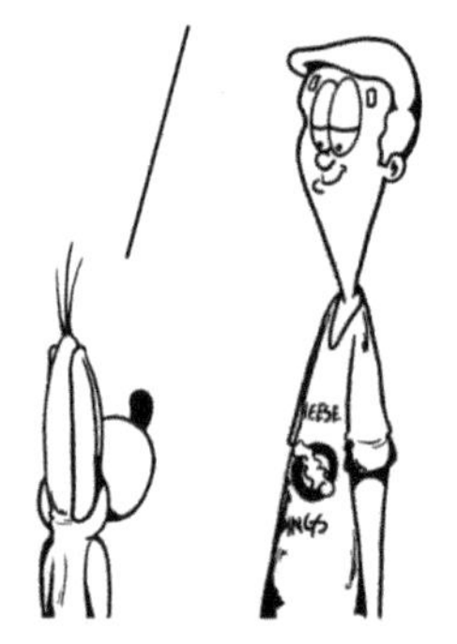

I DON'T HAVE MUCH TIME... I'D BETTER GET PACKED.
WAIT... YOU DON'T WEAR CLOTHES.

AW CRAP... THE SHOW HASN'T EVEN STARTED AND I'M ALREADY THE "ANNOYING NAKED GUY."
WELCOME TO MY REALITY SHOW.

SID ARRIVES IN CALIFORNIA.
WELL THIS SEEMS LIKE A STRANGE PLACE FOR THE CAST TO MEET...

HELLO LITTLE FELLA, YOU MUST BE SID! MY NAME IS TED, AND I'M THE PRODUCER OF THE SHOW.

WHAT'S WITH THE CAMERA?
I'M ALSO CAMERMAN. THEY KEEP THE BUDGET TO A MINIMUM ON THESE REALITY SHOWS.

WELL, AT LEAST WE'RE NOT SHOOTING IN ONE OF THESE HOUSES. AM I RIGHT?
FUNNY YOU SHOULD MENTION THAT...

WELCOME TO YOUR HOME FOR THE NEXT 8 WEEKS.
THERE MUST BE SOME MISTAKE.

OH THERE IS NO MISTAKE... THIS IS WHERE WE'RE GOING TO FILM THE SHOW.
IT JUST DOESN'T SEEM VERY SAFE.

TRUST ME, OUR STAFF HAS CHECKED IT FROM TOP TO BOTTOM.
HEY TED, I FOUND A BALLOON FILLED WITH COCAINE AND A PISTOL IN A SHOE IN MY ROOM.
WELL OKAY.

SID, THIS IS ARTHUR HE IS ONE OF YOUR ROOM-MATES.
HI, YOU HAVE A NEEDLE IN YOUR HEAD.
YEAH... WATCH WHERE YOU SLEEP AROUND HERE.

The rat in the first panel wound up stealing my wallet.

ARE ALL OF THE REALITY SHOWS LIKE THIS?
NOTICE OF FORECLOSURE
LIKE WHAT?
LITE BRITE

WELL, WE LIVE IN A CONDEMNED BUILDING, WE AREN'T GETTING PAID, AND OUR PRODUCER/CAMERAMAN IS SHOOTING THE WHOLE THING ON HIS CAMCORDER.

IT'S WORSE THAN YOU THINK...
HOW SO?
LITE

WE'RE ON UPN.
OH SEE NOW THAT IS TOO #$!@% MUCH!
LITE BRIGHT

The United Paramount Network (UPN) ran from 1995-2006, until it merged with The WB and formed the CW Television Network.

WELL I DON'T LIKE HOW THINGS ARE BEING RUN.
THIS IS HOW IT IS IN THE REALITY SHOW BIZ.

NETWORKS REALIZE THAT THEY CAN CUT THE ACTORS, WRITERS, AND RECORD THESE SHOWS ON A SHOE- STRING BUDGET, AND PEOPLE STILL TUNE IN BY THE TRUCKLOADS.

PLUS WE'LL ALWAYS HAVE CONTESTANTS, BECAUSE EVERYBODY AND THEIR DOG WANTS TO BE ON TV.
WELL YEAH, I JUST...

HOW LONG YOU BEEN SAVING THAT LITTLE GEM?
APPARENTLY NOT LONG ENOUGH.

I can't tell for sure, but I think the Director has a Spongebob shirt on.

MAN, I GOTTA' MAKE DALE THINK EVERYTHING IS FINE, OTHERWISE I'LL NEVER HEAR THE END OF IT.

DEAR DALE, OF ALL OF THE CRACKHOUSES THEY COULD HAVE CHOSEN TO SHOOT THIS SHOW, THIS IS THE BEST. WE TOOK THE BOARDS OFF OF ALL OF THE WINDOWS, AND THAT HAS HELPED A BUNCH WITH THE SMELL.

OUR PRODUCER SAYS THAT THEY'VE FOUND THE LAST OF THE SYRINGES, AND THE RATS SHOULD BE CAUGHT IN NO TIME. SHOOTING STARTS ON MONDAY.... SPEAKING OF SHOOTING, REMIND ME TO TELL YOU A FUNNY STORY WHEN I GET HOME.
YOUR PAL, SID

I JUST REALIZED THAT I LOSE ALL SENSE OF SUBTLETY IN BAD SITUATIONS.

DEAR DALE,
THINGS ARE GOING WELL HERE IN CALIFORNIA.

THE HOUSE IS REALLY BIG, AND THE MEMBERS OF THE CAST THAT I'VE MET SO FAR HAVE BEEN REALLY NEAT.

SHOOTING STARTS ON MONDAY, AND IT SHOULD BE FUN!
TAKE CARE.
LOVE, SID

P.S. IF MY LETTERS STOP ARRIVING, PLEASE SEND A SWAT TEAM AND PARAMEDICS TO THE ADDRESS BELOW.

MAN I REALLY MISS SID.
JOHNSON

IT IS TRUE WHAT PEOPLE SAY... YOU DON'T REALIZE HOW MUCH YOU MISS SOMEONE UNTIL THEY'RE GONE.

FYI - I JUST WAXED OFF THE LAST OF THE POP-TARTS.

SID! WHAT IN THE HECK ARE YOU DOING HERE?
I GOT VOTED OFF AFTER 47 MINUTES. I GUESS IT IS SOME KIND OF RECORD OR SOMETHING.

YOU GOT VOTED OFF OF A REALITY SHOW AFTER 47 MINUTES? IS THAT EVEN POSSIBLE?
IT'S ALL POLITICS, DALE.
JOHNSON

POLITICS?
I MADE A COUPLE OF MISTAKES RIGHT OFF THE BAT AND THEY JUST NEVER GAVE ME A SECOND CHANCE.

ONE PERSON DIDN'T LIKE ME, THEY FORMED AN ALLIANCE, MORE JOINED IN, THEY CALLED AN IMPROMPTU VOTE, AND I WAS SENT PACKING.

SO YOU WERE KIND OF LIKE THE GRAY DAVIS OF THE HOUSE.
THANKS... LIKE I WASN'T DEPRESSED ENOUGH ALREADY.

WELL EVEN THOUGH THE REALITY SHOW THING DIDN'T WORK OUT, I'M GLAD TO HAVE YOU HOME.
REALLY?

YOU BET. I MISSED YOU QUITE A BIT.
MAN, THAT IS REALLY NICE, DALE.

YOU HAVE CHEETO DUST ON THE CORNER OF YOUR MOUTH.
AND YOU HAVE AN INCREDIBLE KNACK FOR KILLING A TENDER MOMENT.

Dale's shirt features a character from "Squaresville," which was my favorite webcomic at the time.

MAN, SID IS REALLY IN A FUNK OVER THIS REALITY SHOW.
JOHNSON

NOTHING A BATCH OF HOT DOG EGGNOG CUPCAKES WON'T FIX. CRAP... THERE IS EGGNOG ALL OVER THE FLOOR. I HAD BETTER...
SEXY CHEF

SEXY CHEF
FOOP!
CRASH!

DO YOU SUPPOSE MARTHA STEWART'S DOG HAS A SIMILAR STORY TO TELL?.

MAN IT HAS BEEN BUSY AROUND HERE LATELY.
MAYBE YOU SHOULD HIRE AN ASSISTANT.
JOHNSON

BUT WHERE WOULD I FIND SOMEONE I COULD PUT THAT LEVEL OF TRUST IN?

SOMEONE I WOULDN'T NEED TO KEEP TRACK OF ALL THE TIME.

SOMEONE WHO... WHAT THE HECK IS WRONG WITH YOU?
I WAS TRYING TO DRAW ATTENTION TO MYSELF, BUT I THINK I THREW MY BACK OUT.

I really do wonder how many sandwiches I've drawn in my lifetime.

I JUST DON'T KNOW IF YOU'D MAKE A GOOD ASSISTANT.
COME ON. I COULD DO THE SIMPLE STUFF THAT YOU DON'T HAVE TIME FOR.
JOHNSON

YOU HAVE A HARD TIME GETTING OFF A PARK BENCH.
YEAH, BUT I CHANGE A MEAN LIGHTBULB.

OKAY, KIDDO, I'LL GIVE YOU A SHOT!
OH MAN! I BET THIS IS HOW TONTO FELT THE DAY THE LONE RANGER HIRED HIM!

WELL MOUNT UP, TONTO, THE TOILET IN 12F HAS BEEN TERRORIZING THE LOCALS.

Someone commented that the way I drew this strip makes it look like Sid and Bob float off into the sky as they talk.

WHAT IN THE HECK ARE YOU WEARING?
I WORK FOR BOB NOW!

DOING WHAT?
FIXING DRYERS, UNCLOGGING DRAINS... YOU KNOW... JANITOR STUFF.

BUT YOU DON'T KNOW HOW TO DO THAT STUFF.
I KNOW... I'M GOING TO BE SELF-TAUGHT, JUST LIKE BOB.
JOHNSON

NOW *THIS* CONCERNS ME.
WHAT CONCERNS ME IS THAT I CAN'T REMEMBER IF THIS CAME OUT OF THE FRIDGE OR THE DISHWASHER.

SO TO RECAP... NO MORE WORKING ON OUR APPLIANCES, AND YOU CAN'T JUST FLUSH TOOLS DOWN THE TOILET AFTER THEY GET DIRTY.
GOT IT.
JOHNSON

GOOD. HERE... I GOT YOU SOMETHING.
WHAT IS IT?

JUST OPEN IT... YOU'LL SEE.
HOW EXCITING!

"SO YOU'VE GONE AND LIT YOURSELF ON FIRE: A BEGINNER'S GUIDE TO HOME REPAIRS AND THE INJURIES THAT ACCOMPANY THEM"
MAN, THIS IS GONNA' COME IN *REAL* HANDY!

Another fan favorite, this one was eventually printed, framed, and given away as part of a contest.

SID, I JUST GOT MY CREDIT CARD BILL...
OH NO.
JOHNSON

IT SEEMS THERE IS A CHARGE TO THE TUNE OF $769 ON HERE FOR AN EBAY AUCTION OF SOME EDDIE MONEY JUNK.
I CAN EXPLAIN.

GO AHEAD, I'M LISTENING.
I... UH... **LOOK!** RICHARD SIMMONS DOING JUMPING JACKS ON OUR LAWN!

YOU REALLY NEED TO LEARN TO PICK THINGS THAT I WOULD ACTUALLY WANT TO TURN AROUND FOR.
IT WAS HIM OR BRITNEY SPEARS. I PANICKED.

Still unhappy with Dale's face and head design, I decided to craft an entire storyline with the single purpose of giving me an excuse to give him a major overhaul.

HOW DID YOU MANAGE TO FIND SOMETHING RELATED TO EDDIE MONEY THAT IS WORTH $769?
THAT'S NOT FUNNY.

I PURCHASED WHAT HAPPENS TO BE THE MOST EXTENSIVE COLLECTION OF BOOTLEG EDDIE MONEY CDS IN ALL OF NORTH AMERICA.

HOW MANY IS THAT?
683... ALL RECORDINGS OF VARIOUS SHOWS THROUGHOUT HIS CAREER.

WHERE IN THE HECK HAVE YOU BEEN HIDING 683 CDS?
MINI-STORAGE. SEE, IT'S RIGHT THERE ON LINE #24.

SID, I AM SO DISAPPOINTED IN YOU.
I'M SORRY, DALE. YOU KNOW I'M WEAK.

I DO. I ALSO KNOW YOU NEED TO BE PUNISHED.
I KNOW.

THEN YOU COME UP WITH YOUR OWN PUNISHMENT.
I COULD TAKE THE CDS TO YOUR STATION AND AUCTION THEM OFF FOR CHARITY.

I SAID PUNISH YOU. NOT MY LISTENERS.
OH, HARDY HAR.

THIS IS THE LAST OF EM'.
I CAN'T BELIEVE YOU TALKED ME INTO THIS.
KHNW
JOHNSON

COME ON. WE'RE MAKING THE BEST OF A BAD SITUATION.
OF ***YOUR*** BAD SITUATION.

WELL, I THINK I'LL GO FOR A WALK AND REFLECT ON THE 2 GLORIOUS DAYS THAT I OWNED THE DEFINITIVE EDDIE MONEY BOOTLEG COLLECTION.

BE STRONG. IT'S WHAT EDDIE WOULD WANT.
TRUST ME... THAT'S THE ***ONLY*** THING KEEPING ME GOING RIGHT NOW.

MAN, LOOK AT ALL OF THESE CDS. IT'S ACTUALLY KIND OF CREEPY BEING SURROUNDED BY EDDIE MONEY LIKE THIS.

I CAN'T BELIEVE I USED TO BE A FAN OF THIS GUY... WAIT... PORTLAND 89? I WAS AT THAT CONCERT! I HAVE GOT TO HEAR THIS ONE.
JOHNSON
CRASH

DALE?
UHHHHHHHH...
TO BE CONTINUED...

I remember the stacks of CDs taking a long time to draw.

DOCTOR, WE'VE GOT A CODE BLUE STAT WITH A NINER VENTRICLE HEMOGLOBIN... WE NEED RHEUMATOID SUPPORT AND A FEMUR SPLEEN SPLICER!!
JOHNSON

WHAT?
YOU'VE BEEN WATCHING "ER" ON YOUR BREAKS AGAIN, HAVEN'T YOU?.

HOW'S THIS - THE GUY IN OPERATING ROOM 12 HAD A BUNCH OF EDDIE MONEY CDS FALL ON HIM, AND HE COULD DIE.
TRY AND WRITE THAT $!@#%, MICHAEL CRICHTON!

This one got me some emails because of how tall and skinny every character I drew was becoming. They were right, so for the next few strips, I focused on short, fat characters.

PLEASE HELP! I'M LOOKING FOR MY FRIEND... I THINK HE'S BEEN IN AN ACCIDENT!
DOCTORS RULE!
JOHNSON

NOW JUST CALM DOWN, SUGAR. DO YOU KNOW WHAT HE WAS BROUGHT IN FOR?

THEY SAID THERE WAS AN ACCIDENT AT HIS RADIO STATION...
OH! THE GUY WHO WAS CRUSHED BY THE EDDIE MONEY CDS... ROOM 18.
DOCTORS RULE!

...AND THEN HE LOCKED HIMSELF IN THE BATHROOM STALL.
I'LL CALL ANIMAL CONTROL.

I'm pretty sure the poster on the wall said, "Mr. Spleen," but then got covered up by the text.

DOCTOR! IS DALE OKAY?
I'M NOT GOING TO SUGAR-COAT THINGS HERE, SON, HE'S IN PRETTY BAD SHAPE.
JOHNSON

BUT HE'S GOING TO MAKE IT, RIGHT?
HE SHOULD MAKE A FULL RECOVERY...

OH, THANK GOODNESS!
...BUT HE'LL NEVER LOOK THE SAME AGAIN.

LIKE IN A POST-OP MELANIE GRIFFITH SORT OF WAY OR A POST-OP JOAN RIVERS SORT OF WAY?
WHICH IS WORSE?
GOOD POINT.

AS YOU CAN SEE, DALE HAD A SERIES OF CDS LODGED *DIRECTLY IN HIS SKULL*.
THAT LOOKS PAINFUL.
JOHNSON

WE HAD HIM HEAVILY SEDATED. HE COULDN'T FEEL A THING... HECK HE COULD HARDLY *MOVE*.
OH GOOD.
DOCTOR GUY!

BUT EVERY ONCE IN A WHILE, HE WOULD COME TO AND MAKE A STRANGLING MOTION...
HANG ON... A WHAT?
DOCTOR GUY!

THEN HE'D SAY, "DOG... MUST... BE PUNISHED" AND PASS OUT AGAIN.
SO THESE PAINKILLERS... CAN I PICK THESE UP AT 7-ELEVEN OR SOMETHING?

OH, DALE... I DON'T KNOW IF YOU CAN HEAR ME, BUT I'M REALLY SORRY ABOUT THIS CD THING...
JOHNSON

...AND FOR GETTING US THROWN IN JAIL, AND MAKING YOU A CAKE WITH SQUIRRELS IN IT, AND...
BEEP!
BEEP!
BEEP!

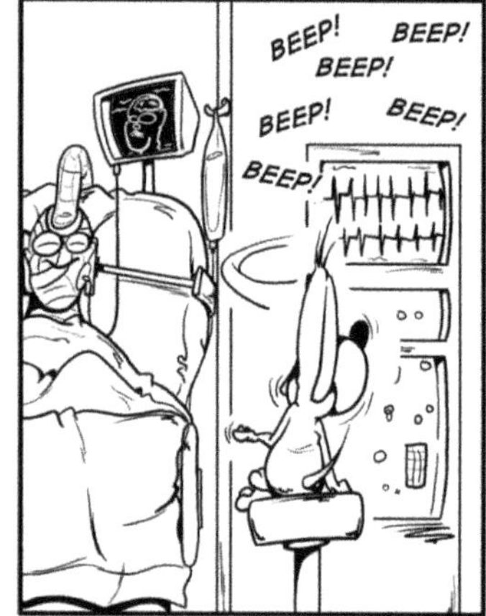
BEEP! BEEP! BEEP! BEEP! BEEP! BEEP!

I'M GUESSING BY HOW FAST THAT THINGAMAJIG IS BEEPING THAT VISITING HOURS ARE OVER. I'LL SHOW MYSELF TO THE DOOR.
BEEP! BEEP! BEEP! BEEP! BEEP!

GOD, COULD YOU PLEASE MAKE SURE THAT MY BUDDY, DALE, MAKES A SPEEDY RECOVERY?
ST GREEN HOSPITAL
JOHNSON

IF YOU DO, I'LL NEVER ASK ANOTHER FAVOR, I SWEAR.

CAN YOU ALSO BRING BACK THAT DOG FOOD WHERE YOU ADD WATER AND IT MAKES GRAVY? OKAY... THAT'S IT, I SWEAR.

I drew this strip, and decided I didn't like the layout...

GOD? COULD YOU PLEASE MAKE SURE THAT MY BUDDY, DALE, MAKES A SPEEDY RECOVERY?
ST GREEN HOSPITAL
JOHNSON

IF YOU DO, I'LL NEVER ASK ANOTHER FAVOR... *I SWEAR*.
ST GREEN

ST GREEN

COULD YOU ALSO BRING BACK THAT DOG FOOD WHERE YOU ADD WATER AND IT MAKES MAKES THE GRAVY? OKAY... *THAT'S* IT, I SWEAR.
ST GREEN

...so I changed it to this. Looking back on it, I don't really know why I did. That first one is actually fine, and I guess I just had lots of free time back then.

JUST THINK, DALE! IN A MATTER OF DAYS, WE'LL GET TO SEE THE NEW YOU!
JOHNSON

YOU MUST BE REALLY EXCITED... YOU COULD END UP LOOKING LIKE BRAD PITT!

OF COURSE, YOU COULD ALSO LOOK LIKE ABE VIGODA WITH A BAD HAIRCUT, BUT TRY AND KEEP YOUR CHIN UP.

IF YOU EVEN HAVE A CHIN... IT'S REALLY HARD TO TELL.

...AND WE'LL JUST TAKE THE LAST OF THE BANDAGES OFF HERE...
THIS SURE IS EXCITING!
JOHNSON

...AND VIOLA!
WOW! DALE, YOU LOOK TOTALLY DIFFERENT. YOU SORT OF LOOK LIKE LIONEL RICHIE.

I AM LIONEL RICHIE.
OH MY LORD! WHY DIDN'T YOU TELL ME?!?

I COULDN'T. I WAS ALL WRAPPED UP.
WELL NEXT TIME TRY AND BANG IT OUT ON A BEDPAN IN MORSE CODE OR SOMETHING!

We never did find out why Lionel was all wrapped in bandages.

THIS IS TERRIBLE. I SPENT THE LAST FEW WEEKS IN A ROOM WITH LIONEL RICHIE, RATHER THAN AT DALE'S SIDE.
JOHNSON

I'VE GOT TO BE THE WORST DOG IN THE WHOLE WORLD.

I HAVE TO SCOUR EVERY INCH OF THIS HOSPITAL UNTIL I FIND HIM, AND I WON'T STOP UNTIL I DO.

I DON'T KNOW WHY HOSPITAL FOOD GETS SUCH A BAD RAP, THESE FISH STICKS ARE AWESOME!

WOW! IF YOU PUT THE FISH STICK IN THE JELL-O, IT TASTES LIKE...
SID?
JOHNSON

I'M SORRY, MISTER... THOSE FISH STICKS WERE STUCK TOGETHER, I SWEAR... I JUST...
IT'S ME... DALE.

REALLY? DALE?!?!
YUP... HOW YOU DOING BUDDY? GIVE ME A HUG.

WAIT JUST A MINUTE... HOW DO I KNOW YOU'RE NOT LIONEL RICHIE?
THAT IS THE STRANGEST THING YOU HAVE EVER SAID.

I finally found a head design I liked. Right? Dale's head would go through at least 3 more major changes over the life of the strip.

DALE, I CAN'T BELIEVE IT'S *YOU!*
IT'S ME. WHERE HAVE YOU BEEN?
PETS
OWED
JOHNSON

LET'S SEE... THE BATH-ROOM STALL, THE X-RAY LAB, LIONEL RICHIE'S ROOM...
FORGET IT. I'M JUST GLAD YOU'RE SAFE.

I MISSED YOU, SID.
I MISSED YOU, DALE.
PETS
OWED

I GOT YOU A GET WELL CARD, BUT LIONEL ASKED TO KEEP IT. HE SAID IT'S THE CLOSEST THING TO FANMAIL HE'S RECEIVED IN OVER A DECADE.
OWED

I CAN'T GET OVER HOW DIFFERENT YOU LOOK.
JOHNSON

YOU LOOK MUCH BETTER!
I DIDN'T KNOW I LOOKED BAD BEFORE.
FRESH
ABIES

NOT BAD... JUST SORT OF LIKE A BALLOON WITH A BAD HAIRCUT.
HOW COME YOU NEVER TOLD ME?
ABIES

YOU LOOKED SO WEIRD... I JUST DIDN'T WANT TO POUR SALT ON THE WOUND.
WELL YOU'RE SURE HEAPING IT ON NOW!!!

"Fresh Babies"

IT IS SO GOOD TO BE HOME.
I'M WITH YOU.
AC/DC
JOHNSON

I'M GOING TO RELAX AND WATCH A LITTLE TV.
I'M TAKING A BATH. WHERE DO WE KEEP THE STEEL WOOL?

THIS WHOLE LIONEL RICHIE THING IS STILL BOTHERING YOU, ISN'T IT?
A LITTLE BIT. DO WE HAVE ANY BLEACH?

The flower sofa and AC/DC picture on the wall speak volumes about Dale.

HEY EVERYONE! IT'S ME, SID! LISTEN, I REALLY WANT YOU TO KNOW THAT YOUR DONATIONS WENT TO A REALLY GOOD CAUSE.

YOUR CASH WAS SPENT ON THINGS NECESSARY TO KEEP THIS STRIP RUNNING, AND NOT A DIME OF IT WAS *WASTED*.

YOU CAN BE ASSURED THAT... *HEY!* WE'RE ALL OUT OF CHAMPAGNE AGAIN! *SOMEONE IS GETTING FIRED THIS TIME!*
JOHNSON

AGAIN, FEEL SAFE KNOWING YOUR MONEY WASN'T WASTED.
HEY, *HEFNER*, ANOTHER CASE OF YOUR SILK UNDERPANTS JUST SHOWED UP.

This was right around the time of the name change from "Dead Air" to "Dog Complex," so to fund the new site, I offered access to this exclusive comic for those who donated.

DALE? ARE YOU SLEEPING?
I SHOULD HAVE GOT A GOLDFISH.
I always liked drawing Sid climbing up on stuff.

WHAT TIME IS IT, SID?
IT'S 3:30... WE NEED TO TALK.

GO AWAY, SID.
I KNOW WE DON'T HAVE A LOT OF MONEY, BUT WE REALLY SHOULD GET EACH OTHER CHRISTMAS GIFTS.

FINE, I'D LIKE A MUZZLE AND A CRATE POSTMARKED FOR CHINA.
YOU CAN BE SO GRUMPY IN THE MORNING.

SID, I DON'T NEED A GIFT.
CAN I MAKE YOU SOMETHING?
CHOCO-COOK

LIKE THE TIME YOU TRIED TO MAKE ME A SPACE SHIP?
I WAS THIS CLOSE.

SID, YOU SPOT-WELDED A GARBAGE CAN TO OUR CAR.
IT'S A ROCKET BOOSTER.

HERE'S 20 BUCKS. DON'T GET ME SOCKS.
WELL YOU'RE NOT GOING TO MAKE THIS EASY, ARE YOU?

NEVER FAILS...
RING!!!

OH HI, DANNY. NO, I'M NOT COMING IN TO WORK UNTIL AFTER THE FIRST OF THE YEAR.

SID? HE'S DOING FINE. HE'S OUT SHOPPING FOR A CHRISTMAS GIFT FOR ME NOW.

ATCH BARN
WELL I'M NOT EVEN SURE WHAT A ROLEX IS, BUT 20 BUCKS IS STILL MY FINAL OFFER.

THIS WAS A GOOD DAY. I GOT DALE A GIFT AND HAD A LITTLE LEFT FOR SOME DECORATIONS.
OPE

OH HI, SANTA!
GIVE OR DIE
DING
DING
DING

I GOT DALE'S GIFT, SO YOU CAN SKIP OUR HOUSE THIS YEAR.
YIPEE.
GIVE OR DIE

YOU CAN JUST... SANTA, ARE YOU WEARING REEBOKS?
I SHOULD HAVE GONE TO LAW SCHOOL.

SHOULDN'T YOU BE GETTING READY FOR THE ***BIG DAY***?
GIVE ME A BREAK, KID, I'M JUST TRYING TO MAKE A LITTLE CASH.
JOHNSON

AREN'T WE ALL? SAY... WHERE ARE YOUR REINDEER?
I SOLD THEM TO PAY RENT.

REALLY? WHAT ABOUT MRS. CLAUS?
SHE MOVED TO SAN DIEGO WITH MY CHIROPRACTOR.

WELL WE KNOW WHO'S MAKING THE NAUGHTY LIST THIS YEAR. ***AM I RIGHT?***
CAN SOMEONE GET THIS THING AWAY FROM ME?!?

MERRY CHRISTMAS, DALE! WOULD YOU LIKE TO OPEN YOUR GIFT NOW?
SURE! I GOT YOU A LITTLE SOMETHING TOO.
NO WAY!
OPEN IT!
A SCARF AND STUFF! ***THANKS, DALE!***
THEY'RE MADE FROM SCANDINAVIAN GOATS, SO THEY'RE EXTRA WARM.
NEAT! THESE ARE SURE GOING TO COME IN HANDY!
GOOD.
NOW YOU! ARE YOU EXCITED?
I SURE AM!
I GOT YOU ***"SHAKES THE CLOWN"!!*** IT'S A COMEDY ABOUT A DRUNKEN CLOWN PLAYED BY BOBCAT GOLDTHWAIT. THE GUY AT THE DVD STORE SAID IT'S ***HILARIOUS***.
BOBCAT GOLDTHWAIT
JULIE BROWN
SHAKES THE CLOWN
UH... I LOVE IT! THANKS, SID.
MERRY CHRISTMAS, DALE!
UM, DALE?
YES, SID?
GOAT FUR GIVES ME HIVES.
I WAS JUST ABOUT TO SAY THE SAME THING ABOUT BOBCAT GOLDTHWAIT.
HAPPY HOLIDAYS!
FROM: DALE, SID, AND ALL THE REST OF THE DEAD AIR CREW!!

WHAT ARE YOU WATCHING, DALE?
I DON'T KNOW... SOME COLLEGE BOWL GAME.
JOHNSON

THE STINK-NO-MORE FOOTSPRAY BOWL?
NAH, I THINK THIS IS THE HANSON'S BEEF AND CHEESE BOWL.

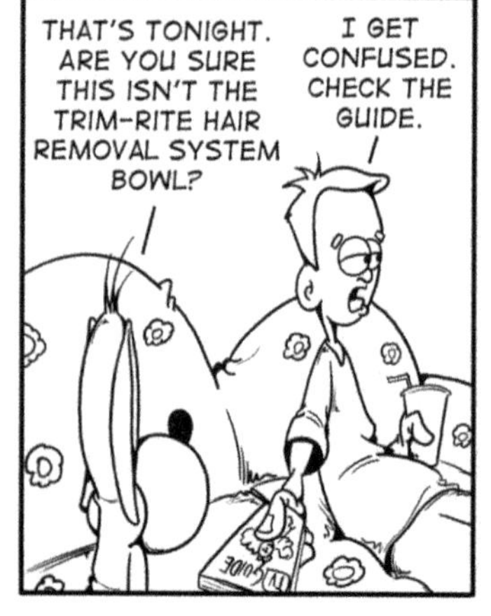
THAT'S TONIGHT. ARE YOU SURE THIS ISN'T THE TRIM-RITE HAIR REMOVAL SYSTEM BOWL?
I GET CONFUSED. CHECK THE GUIDE.
TV GUIDE

MAN, WE WERE WAY OFF. SAYS HERE IT'S "DESIGNING WOMEN."
WRONG DAY, EINSTEIN.

I TOLD YOU YOUR MOM WOULD SEND YOU A GIFT.
YEAH, AND ONLY 5 DAYS PAST CHRISTMAS.
JOHNSON

YOU SHOULDN'T BE SO HARD ON HER.
DON'T DEFEND HER. SHE ISN'T TOO FOND OF YOU.

THAT IS *NOT* TRUE!
LAST YEAR SHE SENT ME A HAIR-WAXING KIT WITH A NOTE THAT SAID "FOR YOUR UNFORTUNATE PROBLEM."

SO?
YOU'RE THE "UNFORTUNATE PROBLEM."

SO YOUR MOM REALLY DOESN'T LIKE ME?
NOT *YOU*... DOGS IN GENERAL.
JOHNSON

BUT THE HAIR REMOVAL KIT SHE SENT YOU LAST CHRISTMAS WAS INTENDED FOR *ME*?
I DIDN'T WANT TO TELL YOU.

AND WHERE DOES SHE THINK I NEED HAIR REMOVED FROM?
YOUR WHOLE BODY. SHE SAYS YOU GET IT ALL OVER.

OH THAT IS RICH! DID SHE EVER THINK IT'S THAT *TOXIC WASTE DUMP OF A PERFUME* SHE WEARS THAT MAKES IT *FALL OFF?!?!*
THIS IS WHY I DIDN'T WANT TO TELL YOU.

Still playing around with styles, I decided to add in some shading. Probably after reading my first "Get Fuzzy" comic strip.

LET'S SEE WHAT MOM SENT.
I STILL CAN'T BELIEVE SHE DOESN'T LIKE ME.

LET'S SEE... LINT ROLLERS, SOME BOTTLES OF FABREEZE, A MUZZLE, HAIR CLIPPERS, AND A MINI-KENNEL. WHY WOULD SHE... *OH NO...*
WHAT'S WRONG?
JOHNSON

SHE'S COMING FOR A VISIT.
I'LL GO PULL THE CAR AROUND, YOU LIGHT THE DRAPES ON FIRE. WE HAVE TO MAKE SURE THERE IS *NO WAY* FOR HER TO TRACE US.

I'M GOING TO STAY WITH BOB WHILE YOUR MOM IS HERE.
NO WAY. SHE WILL SPEND HER VISIT TELLING ME WHAT I'VE DONE WRONG WITH MY LIFE...
JOHNSON

...WHILE SAYING THINGS LIKE, "NOW, FRANK SINATRA, THAT WAS A REAL MAN." I'M *NOT* GOING THROUGH THAT ALONE.
OKAY, BUT IF IT GETS BAD, I'M HIDING IN THE DRYER.

HECK... IF IT GETS *THAT BAD*, I'LL JOIN YOU.
NOT A CHANCE. DRYER LINT MAKES YOU SNEEZE, AND I CAN'T TAKE A CHANCE ON YOU REVEALING MY LOCATION.

This time Dale has a "Lost Sheep" shirt on, which was another of my favorite strips at the time.

IT'S JUST A BATH.
I KNOW, BUT I JUST BATHED LAST WEEK.

YOUR MOM HAD BETTER APPRECIATE IT.
YES, I CAN HEAR IT NOW, "WELL, SON, YOU STILL DON'T HAVE A GIRLFRIEND, AND YOU LIVE IN A TINY APARTMENT, BARELY MAKING ENDS MEET AS A "RADIO JOCKEY," BUT YOUR DOG ROOMMATE IS CLEAN, SO HOW CAN A MOTHER COMPLAIN?"

I always wondered if my chosen shading technique would translate to print. Turns out it does, but only if you look at the pages cross-eyed after hanging upside down for an hour.

DING DONG
AND SO IT BEGINS.

SHE ALWAYS MAKES ME FEEL LIKE SUCH A *CHILD*.
OH, DALE, GIVE HER A CHANCE.

HI, MO...
AREN'T THOSE PANTS A LITTLE *TIGHT* FOR A MAN *YOUR AGE*?
HA! AND YOU THOUGHT SHE WAS GOING TO MAKE YOU FEEL LIKE A CHILD!

Even though Dale's head had been changed via a few Eddie Money CDs and a bit of plastic surgery, I still had to retain the old head shape for his Mom.

CAN I GET YOU ANYTHING, MOM?
HOW ABOUT A SON WHO ISN'T THROWING HIS LIFE AWAY?

GOOD ONE, MOM.
WELL, LOOK AT THAT... YOU *DO* HAVE A PHONE. STRANGE THAT YOU CAN'T EVER SEEM TO CALL ME... IS IT BROKEN?

REALLY, DALE, HOW LONG ARE YOU GOING TO BE IN THERE? I HAVE TO GO.
HUH... I HEAR A DIAL TONE, SO IT MUST BE WORKING...
I TOLD YOU... 4 MORE DAYS.

MRS. FLEMING? DALE SAYS THAT YOU DON'T LIKE ME.
OH HEAVENS NO, DEAR. WHY YOU'RE SWEET ENOUGH...

...TO EAT!!!
AAAAHHHHH!!!!

LOOK AT SID'S LITTLE LEGS KICKING AS HE SLEEPS. MAYBE HE'S DREAMING OF RUNNING THROUGH A MEADOW OR A FIELD OF FLOWERS OR SOMETHING.
ONE CAN ONLY IMAGINE.

SO, MOM, YOU'VE BEEN HERE A FEW DAYS NOW... NOTICE ANYTHING DIFFERENT ABOUT ME?
LET'S SEE... LIVES WITH A DOG, NO GIRLFRIEND, SOCKS ON THE FLOOR... NOPE, NOT A THING.

I MEANT LIKE MY FACE, MOM.
HMMM... WELL... OH MY.... I HADN'T REALLY NOTICED ANYTHING... UM... LET'S SEE...

FACIAL SURGERY, MOM! I'VE HAD COMPLETE RECONSTRUCTIVE FACIAL SURGERY!
NOW THAT YOU MENTION IT, YOU DO LOOK MORE LIKE JOHN TESH THAN WHAT I REMEMBER.

This time Dale is wearing a "Citizen Dog" shirt. You can find books of that comic strip, and I suggest checking them out.

WHAT A HORRIBLE NIGHTMARE, BEING EATEN BY DALE'S MOM.

SOMETHING IN HERE SMELLS GOOD ENOUGH TO EAT! WHAT ARE YOU...
AAAA AAAHHH HH!!!!
PANG!

WHY IS MY MOM ON THE FLOOR?
PROMISE YOU WON'T GET MAD?

WELL THIS WAS MEMORABLE.
HAVE A SAFE DRIVE HOME, MOM.
SORRY FOR THINKING YOU WERE A MONSTER AND HITTING YOU IN THE FACE WITH THAT PAN, MRS. FLEMING.

GET HIM SOME THERAPY BEFORE I COME AGAIN.
AT VERY LEAST I'LL MAKE SURE TO HIDE ALL OUR COOKWARE.
WELL I CAN SEE I'M NEVER GOING TO LIVE THIS ONE DOWN.

I NEED TO HURRY... I'M LATE FOR WORK.
I HAVEN'T HEARD YOU SAY THAT IN A WHILE.

YEAH, IT'S BEEN NICE, BUT I'VE GOT TO GO BACK SOME TIME. WHAT ARE YOU GOING TO DO TODAY?
I'M HAVING LUNCH WITH BOB.

FINE, BUT DON'T COME BACK SPEWING ANY OF HIS PROPAGANDA.
ACTUALLY, I THINK WE'RE HAVING SPAGHETTI.

I really went nuts with mirror reflections for a few strips, didn't I?

DANG, I'M LATE FOR MY LUNCH DATE WITH BOB.
JOHNSON

GO AWAY!!
BOILER RO
KNOCK! KNOCK! KNOCK!
KEEP
STAFF ONLY

HE SAID THE BOILER ROOM... WHY ISN'T HE ANSWERING? BOB? ARE YOU IN...
BOILER ROOM
KEEP OUT!
STAFF ONLY

SWEET CORNBREAD MUFFIN.

THIS IS AMAZING... YET TOTALLY CREEPY. OUR JANITOR HAS SOME KIND OF LAB IN THE BOILER ROOM.
JOHNSON

SID?
AAAHHHH!!!

YOU TRYING TO KILL ME, BOB?!? AND JUST WHAT IN THE HECK IS ALL THIS?
THIS? OH YOU KNOW... PAINT, CLEANERS, MOPS, ALIENS I RESCUED FROM LABS... TYPICAL JANITOR STUFF.

SO YOU RESCUED ALL OF THESE ALIENS FROM LABS YOU WORKED FOR?
YEP!

NEAT!
AND I'M GOING TO DEVELOP A WAY TO SEND THEM ALL HOME!
JOHNSON

BUT YOU COULDN'T EVEN FIGURE OUT WHY OUR TOILET WOULDN'T FLUSH.
I TOLD YOU I WAS HAVING A BAD DAY.

THIS WAS THE FIRST LAUNCHER WE TRIED USING.
"THE ACME ALIEN LAUNCHER."
ACME
JOHNSON

YEAH... I SHOULD HAVE NEVER GONE WITH A STORE-BOUGHT LAUNCHER. WE USED IT ONCE ON A BRAVE LITTLE ALIEN NAMED TED.
WHY ONLY ONCE?

WE SHOT HIM INTO A BRICK WALL AT 500 MILES PER HOUR. IT WAS A SAD DAY, BUT TEDDY KNEW THE RISKS.
AS WOULD ANYONE WHO HAS SEEN A ROADRUNNER CARTOON.

SO BOB, OUR APARTMENT JANITOR, KEEPS ALIENS IN OUR BOILER ROOM.
RIGHT.

WHERE HE HOPES TO DEVELOP A MEANS OF SPACE TRAVEL TO SEND THEM ALL HOME.

RIGHT.

SID, IF BOB DID GIVE YOU SOME KIND OF DRUG, THIS MAN NEEDS TO KNOW.
HE DIDN'T GIVE ME ANY DRUGS!!!
AND HERE I THOUGHT GETTING THAT CAT'S HEAD OUT OF A PICKLE JAR WOULD BE THE HIGHLIGHT OF MY DAY.

HOT DOGS
YOU STILL DON'T BELIEVE ME?!?!
JUST BECAUSE SOME VET SAYS YOU'RE NOT INSANE DOESN'T MEAN I SUDDENLY BELIEVE YOUR ALIENS IN THE BOILER ROOM STORY.

OH WELL FINE. WHEN WE GET BACK TO THE APARTMENT, I'LL SHOW YOU.
I CAN HARDLY WAIT.

IT HURTS RIGHT HERE TO KNOW YOU DON'T BELIEVE ME.
IT HURTS RIGHT THERE BECAUSE THAT WAS YOUR FOURTH CHILIDOG.

SO NOW DO YOU BELIEVE ME?
I CAN'T BELIEVE WHAT I JUST SAW. WE HAVE ALIENS IN OUR BOILER ROOM.

ARE YOU GOING TO TURN BOB IN?
WELL, HIS HEART IS IN THE RIGHT PLACE. IS ALL THAT STUFF SAFE?

OH YEAH. BOB SAID THE FORMER RUSSIAN SCIENTISTS THAT HE BOUGHT THE STOLEN REACTOR FROM WERE VERY REPUTABLE.
AND TO THINK I WAS WORRIED.

HEY, SID, HOW WAS YOUR DAY?
NOT GOOD. I TRIED SELLING LEMONADE TO SOME KIDS.

AT 20 BUCKS A CUP I WAS MAKING GREAT MONEY. THEN THEY FIGURED OUT THAT MY LEMONADE WAS MOSTLY WATER, SO THEY STOLE MY LEMONS.

SO INSTEAD OF LOWERING THE PRICE AND MAKING BETTER LEMONADE, I HIRED A BULLY TO ROUGH UP THE KID WHO STOLE THE MOST LEMONS.
WHERE DID YOU EVER LEARN TO RUN A BUSINESS LIKE THAT?

FROM THIS BOOK.
"HOW TO RUN A BUSINESS THE RECORDING INDUSTRY WAY."

This one still holds true.

KABOOM

GET OUT OF THE WAY!!!!!

NOW CAN I HELP YOU MAKE DINNER?
I TOLD YOU, I CAN HANDLE IT.
SSSSSSSSSS!!!!!

A few people have commented that Sid's actions often mirrored those of my wife. This would be one of those cases.

WE'VE BEEN TOGETHER A LONG TIME, SID.
WE SURE HAVE.

WE'VE GONE THROUGH UPS AND DOWNS...
LOST CHINS AND LOST WEIGHT...

GOOD TIMES AND BAD...
MEATLOAF DOGS AND PRISON TIME...

AND DO YOU KNOW WHAT I'VE COME TO REALIZE?
THAT WE HAVE A REAL LACK OF FEMALE PRESENCE IN OUR LIVES?

YES. WHAT? NO! I MEAN... WELL THAT TOO... BUT I WAS GOING TO SAY THAT YOU'RE A PRETTY DARN GOOD FRIEND.
YOU ARE TOO, DALE.

AND I CAN'T THINK OF ANYONE I'D RATHER LIVE WITH.
SEE, I'D REALLY LIKE TO LIVE WITH THAT GUY WHO INVENTED SNAUSAGES, BUT YOU'RE TOTALLY SECOND.

CAN WE GO SEE A MOVIE?
I DON'T KNOW... EVERY TIME WE GO SOMETHING HAPPENS.

I GET THE KID KICKING MY SEAT, THE TALL GUY IN FRONT OF ME, OR SOMEONE TALKING ON A CELL PHONE RIGHT NEXT TO ME.
OH, NOT EVERY TIME.

LAST TIME I FOUND A PRESS-ON FINGERNAIL IN MY POPCORN.
AND THEY GAVE US A NEW TUB AT HALF PRICE. THAT WAS A PRETTY GOOD NIGHT IF YOU ASK ME.

Dale still holds the high score on that "Death Chicken" machine.

HI, EVERYONE! BOY, YOU READERS SURE HAVE SEEN SOME AMAZING STUFF LATELY...
JOHNSON

FRYING PANS TO THE FACE, HEADS IN POPCORN TUBS, AND KITCHEN FIRES, JUST TO NAME A FEW. BUT THESE WERE ALL PROPS.
RUBBER FLAME CAP PROP USED IN EPISODE #158

LIKE THIS DUMMY WE USED FOR THE BIT YESTERDAY... WHILE IT LOOKS TOTALLY LIFELIKE, IT'S JUST A DUMMY.
I CAN'T BREATHE.

REMEMBER... YOU SHOULD NEVER TRY WHAT YOU READ HERE AT HOME. SOMEONE COULD GET HURT.
SERIOUSLY, I CAN'T FEEL MY EYES.

WE HAVE NEW NEIGHBORS.
REALLY?!? SO THAT'S THE RUCKUS I'VE BEEN HEARING NEXT DOOR.
JOHNSON

SID, THEY HAVE A DOG.
OH NO.
SOD

DALE, WHEN TWO DOGS MEET FOR THE FIRST TIME...
I KNOW, I KNOW...
SOD

"THERE IS A CERTAIN AMOUNT OF SNIFFING THAT TAKES PLACE AND IT MAKES YOU UNCOMFORTABLE."
BINGO.
SOD

YOU MUST BE THE NEW DOG. I'M SID.
I'M BAXTER. NICE TO MEET YOU.
JOHNSON

SO DO YOU LIKE TO DO STUFF ON THE COMPUTER?
SO DO YOU LIKE CHEWING ON STUFF?

Tired of always having to draw Sid on a couch or stool, I decided to give him a friend that was a bit more his own height.

SO, BAXTER, YOU DON'T COOK WITH A MICROWAVE, WATCH TV OR USE A COMPUTER?
NOPE.
BAXTER'S TOYS
JOHNSON

SO WHAT DO YOU DO FOR FUN?
I LIKE TO PLAY FETCH... OH! AND I REALLY LIKE THESE RUBBER NEWSPAPERS! THEY'RE A HOOT!

YOU'RE KIDDING RIGHT?
SEE, IF YOU SQUEEZE EM' THEY SQUEAK! MAN, THESE THINGS ARE A RIOT!
SQUEAK
SQUEAK
SQUEAK
SQUEAK
SQUEAK
SQUEAK
SQUEAK

SID, I FEEL THAT US DOGS SHOULD JUST BE DOGS. WHY DRINK FROM THE GLASS WHEN YOU CAN DRINK FROM THE BOWL?
SODA
JOHNSON

SOME OF US SPEND OUR ENTIRE LIVES TRYING TO BREAK THE MOLD AND BE SOMETHING WE'RE NOT.
DING!
SODA

ME? I'M COMFORTABLE IN MY OWN SKIN.
ME? I'M GONNA' GO GET MY HAM AND CHEESE HOTPOCKET OUT OF THE MICROWAVE!
SODA

BOING!

BOING!
BOING!

WHAM!
JOHNSON

I'M SURE HE DIDN'T MEAN TO, SID, AND IT'S NOT A BARBARIC GAME FOR NEANDERTHAL DOGS. IT'S JUST FETCH. A GAME NORMAL DOGS PLAY. MAYBE YOU SHOULD TRY BEING NORMAL.
OH, YOU'D LIKE THAT, WOULDN'T YOU?

Looking back, it was an odd choice to bill Baxter as such a "dog's dog," and yet still have him run on two legs.

SO YOU DON'T MIND THAT I'M AN INDEPENDENT DOG?
OF COURSE NOT.
JOHNSON

I LIKE THAT YOU'RE INDEPENDENT... JUST LIKE ME. WE CAN TAKE CARE OF OURSELVES.
1A
KNOCK
KNOCK
KNOCK

HI, MS. TREADBOTTOM. MY YOU'RE LOOKING... STUNNING. I'M LOCKED OUT AGAIN.
THAT'S TWICE THIS WEEK. DO IT AGAIN AND I'M STAPLING A KEY TO YOUR HEAD.
GUT BUSTER

Ms. Treadbottom should have been in more strips. In related news, she now works at the Mini-Mart that I fuel up at each week.

SO YOU DON'T MIND THAT I PREFER PLAYING CHECKERS OVER FETCH?
NOT AT ALL.
THE PAPER
JOHNSON

OR WATCHING TV INSTEAD OF CHASING MY TAIL?
NOPE.

OR THAT I PREFER MICROWAVE FROZEN ENTREES TO DOG FOOD FROM A CAN?
MORE POWER TO YOU.

OR THAT I'D RATHER SHAVE MY BODY WITH A CHEESE GRATER AND SOAK IN A BATH OF LEMON JUICE THAN BRING YOU YOUR SLIPPERS AND PAPER?
OKAY, THAT HAS ALWAYS BOTHERED ME.

TODAY'S DOG COMPLEX IS BROUGHT TO YOU BY:
CBS SPORTS
AND
MTV MUSIC TELEVISION
JOHNSON

I AM SO SICK OF HEARING ABOUT JANET JACKSON'S BOOB.
I KNOW. IT WAS ONLY ON SCREEN FOR A SECOND. NO BIG DEAL.

HECK, I'M NAKED WEEK IN AND WEEK OUT AND NOBODY SEEMS TO CARE.
EXACTLY.

HEY, WHY HAVE WE BACKED OUT TO A WIDE SHOT JUST LIKE THE ONE THEY WENT TO AFTER SHOWING JANET'S BOOB?
UH OH.

Janet Jackson's boob fell out during a Superbowl Halftime Show, and for the next month, it was the biggest story on the planet.

ARE WE IN TROUBLE?
WELL, YOU HAVE BEEN WALKING AROUND NAKED.
JOHNSON

I'M A DOG! WE DON'T WEAR CLOTHES!
I HAVE TO GO READ THIS STATEMENT TO THE PRESS.

LET ME SEE THAT.
OKAY, BUT REMEMBER, I DIDN'T WRITE IT.

OH YOU HAVE GOT TO BE KIDDING. A COSTUME MALFUNCTION? I DON'T WEAR A COSTUME!
KEEP YOUR ROBE ON, CHIEF, THIS IS A FAMILY STRIP.

AND NOW, A WORD FROM DALE FLEMING
I'M SORRY IF ANYONE WAS OFFENDED BY SID'S RECENT CHOICE IN WARDROBE, OR LACK THEREOF...
JOHNSON

I WAS SHOCKED AS I'M SURE MOST OF THE READERS WERE, BUT I WANT TO MAKE THIS POINT CLEAR...

THIS WAS AN UNFORTUNATE COSTUME MALFUNCTION, AND STEPS HAVE BEEN MADE TO ASSURE IT NEVER HAPPENS AGAIN.
FOR THE LAST TIME, I DO NOT WEAR A @!#$%& COSTUME!
CENSORED

THE FALLOUT FROM "SIDGATE"
NO WAY AM I WEARING THIS.
I THINK WE LOOK KIND OF CUTE.
LIL' ANGEL
STUD
JOHNSON

SOME WERE PUT ON TAPE DELAY
I'M NOT EVEN SURE WHAT A TAPE DELAY IS.
THIS IS SO STUPID. WE DON'T EVEN USE A @#& TAPE!

SOME SOUGHT AFFECTION
I NEED A HUG.
NOT WITH BIG BROTHER WATCHING.
YEAH, NO WAY DUDE.

OTHERS STOOD DEFIANT
CENSOR THIS, BUCKO!!!
CENSORED
CENSORED

Apologies to Mr. Conley, Mr. Pastis, and Mr. Thompson.

I DON'T THINK THIS COULD GET ANY WORSE.
IT JUST DID.
SODA
JOHNSON

SAYS HERE THE SENATE IS HOLDING HEARINGS NEXT WEEK. THEY WANT TO TALK TO YOU.
WAIT... AS IN *THE* SENATE? I CAN'T DO THIS. ***NO WAY.***
SODA

I DON'T EVEN HAVE ANYTHING TO WEAR.
THAT'S WHAT THEY WANT TO TALK TO YOU ABOUT.
SODA

YES, BUT SEE, I'M ALWAYS NAKED.
TODAY'S HEARING: NUDITY IN COMIC STRIPS
JOHNSON

WELL NO, I DON'T THINK IT'S WRONG. I'M A DOG. DOGS DON'T WEAR CLOTHES.

WHY? WELL, ON ACCOUNT OF OUR SHORT LIMBS. CLOTHES JUST DON'T FIT DOGS.

WELL YES, I COULD TRY SHOPPING WHERE YOUR HUSBAND DOES. GOOD ONE, MRS. CLINTON.

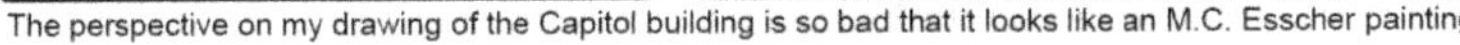
The perspective on my drawing of the Capitol building is so bad that it looks like an M.C. Esscher painting.

SENATORS, IS SEEING ME WITHOUT CLOTHES ***REALLY THAT BIG OF A DEAL?***
JOHNSON

I THINK WE ***ALL*** HAVE BETTER THINGS WE SHOULD BE FOCUSING OUR ATTENTION ON.

NOW LET'S ALL GET A LIFE AND STOP WORRYING ABOUT ***A LITTLE SKIN***, SHALL WE?

ONE MORE THING... CAN SENATOR KENNEDY PLEASE STOP WINKING AT ME? IT'S REALLY STARTING TO CREEP ME OUT.

I'M GLAD YOU WERE ALLOWED TO CONTINUE WORKING IN YOUR ***NATURAL STATE.***
THEY FINALLY SAW IT MY WAY.
JOHNSON

AND THEY DIDN'T EVEN MAKE YOU WEAR PANTS.
HUH... YOU KNOW WE DIDN'T REALLY DISCUSS THE LOWER HALF OF MY BODY.

WE'RE BACK TO A WIDE SHOT.
OH NO.

WANNA' SURF THE WEB?
NAH. WANNA' SNIFF SOME STUFF?

NAH. WANNA' PLAY LAWN DARTS?
NAH. WANNA' CHASE A CAT?

NAH. WANNA' WATCH MY "GILLIGAN'S ISLAND" DVD?
NAH... WAIT... WHAT?

JUST SIT RIGHT BACK AND YOU'LL HEAR A TALE, A TALE OF A FATEFUL TRIP...
GLAD TO SEE YOU TWO HAVE FOUND SOME COMMON GROUND.

IN A WAY GILLIGAN'S ISLAND REPRESENTS MY OWN STRUGGLE TO BREAK FREE OF THE DOG STEREOTYPE.

THEY ALWAYS MAKE A PLAN TO GET OFF THE ISLAND, BUT IT ALWAYS GETS MESSED UP.

I TRY AND BE MORE THAN A DOG, BUT SOMETHING ALWAYS HAPPENS THAT I DON'T EXPECT AND...

SNAUSAGE?
HECK YES! I LOVE THESE THINGS!

SID! GUESS WHERE WE'RE GOING?
A STUPID HAT CONVENTION?

Sid was starting to get pretty good at the whole "art thing."

FUNNY STUFF. NO, WE'RE GOING CAMPING!
REALLY?

I THOUGHT WE'D HANG OUT WITH MOTHER NATURE FOR A FEW DAYS.
OR AS I LIKE TO CALL HER, THE ONLY WOMAN THAT WON'T TURN YOU DOWN FOR A DATE.

CAN I INVITE BAXTER ON OUR CAMPING TRIP?
SURE!

MAN, THIS IS GOING TO BE GREAT! CAN WE MAKE S'MORES TOO?
YOU BET.

COOL! I'LL MAKE SURE TO PACK THE MUSTARD.
YOU HAVE NO IDEA WHAT S'MORES ARE, DO YOU?

DALE, BAXTER GETS TO COME!
GOOD DEAL!

HE'S NEVER BEEN CAMPING EITHER.
WELL TELL HIM TO GET TO BED EARLY... WE LEAVE AT DAWN.

DAWN? WHY SO EARLY?
I'M GOING TO CATCH US SOME FISH FOR BREAKFAST.

HOW ABOUT I PACK A BOX OF POP-TARTS AND WE LEAVE AROUND NOONISH?
NICE TRY.

Yet another comic strip character on Dale's shirt, this time for "The Fray."

MAN, WE'RE IN THE MIDDLE OF NOWHERE.
ARE WE LOST, DALE?

DO I LOOK LIKE AN IDIOT? MY DAD TOOK ME CAMPING HERE ALL THE TIME, BUT I'LL GO ASK THAT LOGGER JUST TO PUT YOUR MINDS AT EASE.

WHAT DID HE SAY?
HE SAID, "ONLY AN IDIOT COULD HAVE DRIVEN TO CANADA BY MISTAKE."

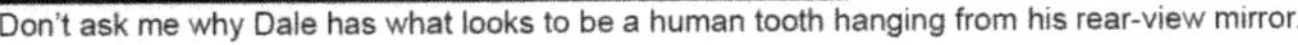
Don't ask me why Dale has what looks to be a human tooth hanging from his rear-view mirror.

WE FINALLY MADE IT.
WOW! SMELL THAT FRESH AIR!

LET'S GET UNPACKED, AND SET UP THE TENT.
WHERE'S THE CABIN?

WHAT CABIN?
WE'RE STAYING IN A CABIN OR HOUSE OR SOMETHING, RIGHT?

SID, WE'RE CAMPING. WHY DO YOU THINK WE BROUGHT THE TENT?
I THOUGHT IT WAS FOR BAXTER.
HEY!

YOU CAN'T EXPECT ME TO SLEEP IN A TENT FOR AN ENTIRE WEEK.
YOU'RE NOT. YOU'RE SLEEPING OUTSIDE.

YOU MEAN... IN THE WILD!?!
C'MON, SID, YOU'RE NOT SCARED, ARE YOU?

SCARED? SCARED?!? LISTEN HERE, SPOT, THE DAY I'M SCARED OF NATURE IS THE DAY...
COOL! A SNAKE!

SEE, SID, IT'S SMALL ENOUGH TO BE A WORM... NOW UNLOCK THE DOORS.
AND LET THAT ANACONDA IN? YEAH... NOT HAPPENING.

I'M GLAD YOU FINALLY GOT OUT OF THE CAR.
FROM THIS POINT ON, I AM A MOUNTAIN DOG.
JOHNSON

GOOD. YOU WANNA' HELP US FINISH GETTING CAMP SET UP?
JUST POINT ME IN A DIRECTION, BOSS, I'M AT ONE WITH NATURE.

WELL, WHY DON'T YOU BOIL SOME WATER TO GO WITH OUR LUNCH?
RIGHT... JUST POINT ME IN THE DIRECTION OF THE THE MICROWAVE.

HOW'S SID DOING?
NOT GOOD. HE HAD NO IDEA CAMPING WAS SO FAR REMOVED FROM THE COMFORTS OF HOME.
JOHNSON

I SORTA FEEL BAD FOR HIM.
OH, DON'T WORRY ABOUT SID... HE'LL ADAPT.

SO YOU'RE TELLING ME THERE IS NO STARBUCKS AROUND HERE ANYWHERE?
WUB WUB WUB

CAMPING STINKS. "ROAST A MARSHMALLOW," HE SAYS, "THAT'LL CHEER YOU UP."
JOHNSON

FWOOM!

I AM SO HANGING RAW MEAT FROM HIS TENT TONIGHT.

OKAY, SID, IF YOU GUYS NEED ANYTHING, I'LL BE IN THE TENT.
GOT IT.

HOWEVER, I WANT YOU TO THINK BEFORE YOU CALL ME.
ROGER THAT.
JOHNSON

FRANKLY, UNLESS A BEAR IS GNAWING ON YOUR BODY, I DON'T CARE.
THANK YOU FOR THE LOVELY VISUAL AS I GO CLIMB INTO MY SLEEPING BAG.

Who draws a moon like that? And someone tell Dale that his tag is sticking out.

BAXTER? ARE YOU SLEEP?
I WAS.

I HAVE TO GO.
GO WHERE?

YOU KNOW... GO!
SO? GO OFF INTO THE BUSHES AND GO.

ALONE?!?
IT'S NEVER REALLY BEEN A TWO DOG JOB FOR ME.

I CAN'T BELIEVE I'M STANDING OUT HERE WITH YOU.
KEEP YOUR EYES PEELED.

FOR WHAT?
CRAZED BEARS WITH CHAINSAWS AND OTHER THREATS OF NATURE.

I SEE A SQUIRREL LICKING HIMSELF. DOES THAT COUNT?
I'M NOT SURE... IF HE CHARGES, CLIMB A TREE. I DON'T THINK SQUIRRELS CAN CLIMB TREES.

ARE YOU DONE?
DO YOU FIND CERTAIN LEAVES TO BE SOFTER THAN OTHERS?

LET'S GET BACK TO CAMP... I'M FREEZING.
I HEAR THAT... LEAD THE WAY.

HANG ON... I THOUGHT YOU KNEW THE WAY.
WHY WOULD I?

IF YOU'RE SERIOUS, I'M THROWING A SNAKE ON YOU AND LETTING DALE FIND US BY THE SOUND OF YOUR SCREAMS.
THAT'S NOT EVEN FUNNY.

I actually got a piece of hate mail that had this strip pasted in it, followed by the words, "Neither is your comic strip."

NOW, CALM DOWN, MR. FLEM.
IT'S FLEMING.

RIGHT, TELL ME WHAT HAPPENED AGAIN?
I TOLD YOU... WHEN I GOT UP, THE TWO DOGS WERE MISSING.

AND YOU SAY THEY'RE IN SEARCH OF A WAFFLE HOUSE?
YEAH... OR A STARBUCKS.

BE HONEST, MR. FLEM, DID YOU SAMPLE ANY LITTLE WILD MUSHROOMS LAST NIGHT?
IT'S FLEMING.

WAIT! I THINK I SMELL DALE!
MAN, AM I GLAD YOU REMEMBERED ABOUT THAT WHOLE KEEN SENSE OF SMELL THING.
JOHNSON

THIS WAY!
WE'RE ALMOST BACK... I CAN FEE... FEE... FEE...

STOP MESSING AROUND, SID, I'M TRYING TO FOCUS.
FEE... FEE... FEE... FEE...
My bears looked more like dogs than my dogs did.

I CAN'T BELIEVE THAT STUPID GAME WARDEN SAID TO WAIT HERE FOR SID AND BAXTER TO SHOW UP.
JOHNSON

AS IF THOSE TWO ARE JUST GOING TO COME WALTZING THROUGH CAMP LIKE...

AAAAAAAAHHHHHHHHH

WHY DO I GET THE SINKING FEELING I SHOULD BE RUNNING WITH THEM?

YOU CAN COME OUT NOW, GUYS, THERE IS NOTHING CHASING YOU.
DALE, CAMPING STINKS. I THINK WE SHOULD GO HOME.
JOHNSON

I HATE TO SAY IT, BUT I AGREE WITH SID.
ARE YOU MAD, DALE?

WHAT KIND OF QUESTION IS THAT? I ASSUME A BEAR DOES THAT IN THE WOODS, BUT WHAT IN THE HECK DOES THAT HAVE TO DO...
IT MEANS "YES."
"Dog Complex" was running in my town's newspaper by the time this one was printed, and they got an angry letter from a Mom who didn't know how to explain the punchline to her kid.

DALE, I'M REALLY SORRY THE CAMPING THING DIDN'T WORK OUT.

THAT'S OKAY.
WELL, I FELT BAD, SO I GOT YOU SOMETHING.
JOHNSON

"COMPUCAMPING"
IT'S A COMPUTER PROGRAM THAT SIMULATES CAMPING!

THAT'S JUST PLAIN RIDICULOUS.
WHAT'S RIDICULOUS IS THAT THEY THREW IN THE POISON OAK BONUS DISC FOR ONLY 9 BUCKS!

HOW'S THE CAMPING SIMULATOR?
IT SAYS I DON'T HAVE ENOUGH MEMORY TO PITCH MY VIRTUAL TENT.
CLICK CLICK

REALLY?
YEAH, AND WHAT DOES "UNEXPECTED FAULT IN MARSHMALLOW.EXE" MEAN?
JOHNSON

"CANNOT FIND LAWNCHAIR.DLL"... WE'D BETTER REBOOT.
I CAN ALMOST SMELL THE CAMP-FIRE BURNING.
ACTUALLY, I THINK THAT'S YOUR HARD DRIVE.

HEY! I KNOW YOU CAN HEAR ME. YOU SEE THIS CALENDAR? IT SAYS TODAY IS THE FIRST DAY OF SPRING, BUT I AIN'T SEEIN' IT. YOU'D BETTER KICK IT IN GEAR, LADY!
JOHNSON

WHAT THE!?!
POP!

AAAAAAAHHHHHHH!!!!
POP! POP! POP! POP! POP! POP! POP! POP!

WHAT HAPPENED?
MOTHER NATURE TRIED TO KILL ME.

My Sister In-Law's favorite strip. This one is for you, Kat.

SHOOT... THE TOAST IS STUCK AND STARTING TO BURN.
RATTLE RATTLE
JOHNSON

DANGIT, NOW THE FORK IS STUCK TOO.
GZZZT!!

SID! YOU PUT A FORK IN THE TOASTER!?! ARE YOU NUTS?!?
OH RELAX... I'M FINE.

YOU ARE SO LUCKY. CATS HAVE NINE LIVES... NOT DOGS.
WELL, UNLESS YOU'VE GOT ONE I CAN JAM IN THE TOASTER, I DON'T REALLY SEE HOW THAT'S RELEVANT.

SID, YOU CAN'T GO AROUND STICKING FORKS IN TOASTERS. YOU NEED TO BE CAREFUL.
OKAY, OKAY. WHY ARE YOU SO BENT OUT OF SHAPE?
JOHNSON

BECAUSE I DON'T KNOW WHAT I'D DO IF I EVER LOST YOU.

YOU'RE STILL IN TROUBLE FOR BREAKING THE TOASTER.
I LOVE YOU TOO, DALE.

By this point, I was getting a decent amount of mail, hardly ever positive. The one I got for this strip read, "We get that you're a sap. No need to draw the tears."

JOHNSON

HEY, YOU WANNA LOCK YOUR DOOR BEFORE YOU GO ALL **LORD OF THE DANCE** NEXT TIME? I'M SCARRED FOR LIFE HERE.

My wife once caught me doing this very thing.

CHECK OUT MY NEW HAT! IT LETS THE WORLD KNOW THAT I ENJOY FEMALE COMPANIONSHIP.
WHERE DID YOU GET **THAT**?
JOHNSON

BAXTER FOUND IT IN THE DUMPSTER.
OH GROSS! SID, TAKE THAT **OFF!**

SO I SUPPOSE YOU'RE NOT GOING TO LET ME KEEP THE TOOTHBRUSH EITHER.
AFTER I BURN THIS, YOU ARE **SO** GETTING A BATH.

SID, COULD YOU... OH HEY, BAXTER. I DIDN'T KNOW YOU WERE COMING OVER.
HIS OWNER HAD TO RUN TO THE STORE.
JOHNSON

WHY IS IT THAT I'VE NEVER **MET** YOUR OWNER?
TELL YOU WHAT... WHEN SHE GETS BACK, I'LL INTRODUCE YOU TO HER.

S-S-**SHE**? H-H-**HER**?
WHOAH... LOOK AT HIS EYE TWITCH.
I CAN ACTUALLY **HEAR** HIS PALMS SWEATING.

Sid had a new friend, so now I felt it was time Dale had one as well.

YOU'RE NOT GOING TO GET **WEIRD** NOW THAT BAXTER'S OWNER IS COMING OVER ARE YOU?
MY HEAD IS **REALLY** MISSHAPEN.
JOHNSON

DON'T START QUESTIONING YOUR APPEARANCE LIKE YOU DO BEFORE A DATE. THIS IS JUST A **FRIENDLY DINNER**.

DO YOU THINK MY RIGHT EYE LOOKS LARGER THAN MY LEFT ONE?

WELL, I HADN'T REALLY NOTICED, BUT...
GOOD LORD, I AM A GENETIC FREAK!

DALE, YOU NEED TO CALM DOWN.
I AM CALM. *YOU'RE NOT CALM*. I'M CALM. HECK I'M *OOZING* CALM.
CHOP
CHOP
CHOP
CHOP

EVER SINCE BAXTER TOLD US HIS OWNER WAS A *GIRL*, YOU'VE BEEN ACTING LIKE A DORK.
I'M JUST CHOPPING UP SOME THINGS FOR OUR DINNER.
CHOP
CHOP
CHOP
CHOP

YOU JUST CHOPPED UP OUR DISH SPONGE.
IT ADDS *TEXTURE* TO THE MEATLOAF, OKAY?

IT'S BEEN A WHILE, BUT WHAT YOU DO IS MAKE THE "AIRPLANE HANGAR" LIKE THIS... NO WAIT... UH... LIKE *THIS*...

THEN YOU FLY THE PLANE UP THROUGH... WELL... YOU... OH *DANGIT*...

SON OF A... WHY WON'T THE PLANE FIT IN THE #@$%& HANGAR!!

I THINK YOUR PILOT'S LICENSE HAS EXPIRED.
JUST GO GET THE SCISSORS. I CAN'T BREATHE.

DANG... I HAVEN'T EVEN PUT THE MEATLOAF IN THE OVEN YET. HOW DO I LOOK?
YOU LOOK FINE.

IS THIS COLOGNE TOO MUCH?
I THINK YOU SMELL NICE.

HOW'S MY HAIR?
MESSY YET PLAYFUL. *NICE WORK*.

DO THESE PANTS MAKE MY *JUNK* LOOK TOO BIG?
AND WITH *THAT* YOU'VE OFFICIALLY CROSSED THE LINE. I'LL BE WATCHING CHARLES IN CHARGE.

OH NO... THE MEATLOAF ISN'T EVEN IN THE OVEN!
DING!
DONG!

I CAN'T GO THROUGH WITH THIS!
YOU'RE JUST STALLING... HAND OVER THE BOWL OF MEAT.

GO ANSWER THE DOOR!
LET GO, SID!!!

HELLO, MY NAME IS DALE, AND I'M THE GUY YOU WILL PURPOSELY AVOID IN THE HALL FROM THIS DAY FORTH.
SEE... I TOLD YOU HE WAS FUNNY.

WOW... YOU'RE STILL HERE.
WHY WOULDN'T I BE?

WELL, I DID GREET YOU AT THE DOOR WEARING MY BEST MEATLOAF.
HEY, ACCIDENTS HAPPEN... ESPECIALLY WITH A DOG AROUND. I'VE GOT SOME STORIES I COULD TELL YOU ABOUT BAXTER TOO.

SID GOT ME THROWN IN JAIL FOR DOWNLOADING PIRATED MUSIC.
WELL THAT BLOWS MY "ATE A HOLE IN MY SLIPPER" STORY OUT OF THE WATER.

WOW, YOU SURE HAVE A NICE DOG!
THANK YOU! HE'S THE BEST!
FINGER

I LIKE MY DOG BUT SID IS MUCH BETTER!
HE SURE IS!
CAT
CHEST HAIR
NO SHIRT

I WILL MARRY YOU IF WE CAN SHIP MY DOG TO CHINA AND KEEP SID!
OKAY!
FAKE NOT REAL
PIE
SID RULES

SO WHAT ARE YOU DRAWING?
NOTHING!

Sid was way better at this comic strip stuff than I ever was.

IN ALL THE EXCITEMENT, I NEVER GOT YOUR NAME.
I'M BETH.

I HAVEN'T SEEN YOU AROUND MUCH, BETH.
OH I'VE SEEN PLENTY OF YOU.

HUH?
SOMEONE SLIPPED THIS PHOTO UNDER MY DOOR A WEEK AGO.

OH MY LORD! THIS IS ME IN MY UNDERWEAR!!!
SINGING INTO A LINT ROLLER TO BE EXACT. VERY ROCKSTAR OF YOU.

SID, I'VE NEVER BEEN SO ANGRY WITH YOU!
WHY?

ANY IDEA WHO TOOK THIS PHOTO OF ME IN MY UNDERPANTS?
OH THAT... YOU WERE ROCKING OUT TO BON JOVI. YOU LOOKED CUTE.

SO YOU TOOK A PICTURE AND STUFFED IT UNDER BETH'S DOOR?!?!
IT'S CALLED AN ICEBREAKER, DALE.

YOU DID LOOK KIND OF CUTE.
I HAVE BEEN WORKING OUT LATE...
THAT IS NOT THE POINT!

DALE SOUNDED ANGRY.
HE'S SORE ABOUT THAT PHOTO I SLID UNDER BETH'S DOOR.
JOHNSON

OF HIM IN HIS UNDERWEAR? I'D BE MAD TOO.
OH, HE JUST TOLD ME NOT TO DO IT AGAIN.

THAT'S IT?!?
I GUESS NOTHING QUELLS A BURNING RAGE QUITE LIKE A WOMAN TELLING YOU THAT YOU LOOK CUTE IN YOUR UNDERPANTS.

IT WAS GREAT TO MEET YOU, BETH.
YOU TOO.

IF YOU EVER NEED YOUR DISPOSAL UNCLOGGED OR ANYTHING, LET ME KNOW.
UMM... OKAAAY.

OH... NO... I MEANT YOUR ACTUAL DISPOSAL... DON'T THINK I MEANT...
GOODNIGHT, DALE.

WELL I THOUGHT THAT WENT WELL.
I'M GOING TO GO CRY MYSELF TO SLEEP.

SO WHAT PART OF "NO HAND TOSSING YOUR OWN PIZZA" DID YOU NOT UNDERSTAND?
I'D BETTER GO GET THE SNOW SHOVEL.
JOHNSON

THE THOUGHT OF THE AFTERLIFE SCARES ME TO DEATH.
JOHNSON

WHEN IT'S MY TIME, WILL MY ACTIONS LAND ME IN A CLOVER FILLED FIELD, CHASING BALLS ALL DAY, DRINKING WATER FROM A GOLDEN TOILET, AND EATING FROM A NEVER-ENDING BOWL OF CANNED DOG FOOD?

SOUNDS WONDERFUL. WHAT DO YOU THINK HELL IS LIKE?
THAT IS MY IDEA OF HELL.

CHAPTER 2: PET SHOPS AND A MAN NAMED, MONKEY

I had made so many changes to "Dead Air," that it was now a mere shell of its former self. Not only that, but most of the characters had run their course for me, outside of Sid and Dale.

So I decided it was time for a change. It was time for Sid and Dale to pack up, and leave the radio station and crazy janitors behind.

I wanted to find Dale a job working with animals, because those were always my favorite characters to draw. The Zoo was my first thought, but it was hard enough to get Sid to fit in a panel with Dale, let alone a bull elephant, so I went with my second choice of a Pet Shop.

Sid wasn't especially thrilled about moving, but when I told him Baxter would still swing by for a visit now and then, he warmed up to the idea.

HEY, DALE! HOW WAS WORK TODAY?
I QUIT.

FOR THE LAST TIME, WE ARE NOT GOING TO HAVE TO LIVE IN OUR CAR.
AND ALL I'M SAYING IS IF WE DO, I GOT DIBS ON BACKSEAT.
COMIC CHANGES STYLE AGAIN

It's been 10 pages, so time for another Dale head. A bit later, Sid will have some fun with all of these noggin swaps.

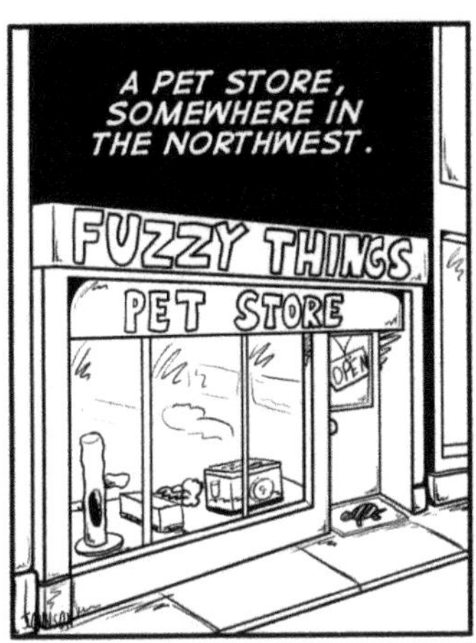
A PET STORE, SOMEWHERE IN THE NORTHWEST.
FUZZY THINGS
PET STORE
OPEN

I'M GOING FOR COFFEE, KEEP AN EYE ON THINGS, WILLY.
BRING ME A DANISH.
FUZZY THINGS

EEERRCCHHH!!!
WHAM!!!

THAT DIDN'T SOUND GOOD.
SO MUCH FOR MY DANISH.
WAR AND PEACE

The introduction of Angus, Willy, and some old guy I drove over with a bus.

EVERYONE, I HAVE TERRIBLE NEWS...

MILTON, THIS STORE'S OWNER AND OUR FRIEND, HAS PASSED AWAY.
HE'S MOVED ON TO THAT BIG PET SHOP IN THE SKY.
1932–2004

HE WENT PEACEFULLY.
HE WAS HIT BY A BUS.
1932–2004

ANGUS! IXNAY ON THE USBAY!
OH YEAH... IT NAILED HIM RIGHT IN THE USBAY.
1932–2004

SO YOU TOLD YOUR BOSS TO TAKE THAT JOB AND SHOVE IT?
HE'S ON VACATION.

BUT YOU TOLD SOMEONE TO SHOVE IT, AM I RIGHT?
I JUST GAVE MY RESIGNATION TO HIS ASSISTANT.

DID YOU SHOVE IT AT HER?
I LAID IT ON HER DESK.

YOU NEED TO WORK ON YOUR SHOVING.
HOW ABOUT I START BY SHOVING YOU OUT OF MY ROOM?

I'M SURE MILTON'S PASSING IS TOUGH ON US ALL... DOES ANYONE HAVE ANY QUESTIONS?
NOT 4 SALE
JOHNSON

GO AHEAD, CHASE.

WILL THEY BE GIVING HIM THE *OL' FLUSHAROO?*

NOW THAT'S JUST *SILLY*. WE ALL KNOW HE'S TOO BIG FOR THE *"OL' FLUSHAROO,"* SO I HAVE TO ASSUME THEY'LL USE A BIG SHOEBOX.

Willy the Parrot used a marker to write "Not 4 Sale" on his own chest. It eventually wore off.

HERE.
WHAT'S THAT?

THE CLASSIFIEDS. I CIRCLED SOME JOBS I THOUGHT YOU MIGHT BE GOOD AT!
LIKE THIS ONE?
HELP WANTED
CLASSIFI
JOHNSON

IT SAYS VOICE TALENT.
I'M *NOT* WORKING FOR 1-900-FUN-BUNS.

WILLY! HAVE YOU HEARD?!?
JOHNSON

I WAS TALKING TO A.C. OUT BACK, AND HE SAID WE'RE ALL BEING SOLD TO SOME *GENETIC LAB!*
ANGUS, I DON'T THINK...

HUMAN EARS, WILLY!!! GROWN RIGHT ON OUR BACKS!!!

MUST YOU GET HIM RILED UP LIKE THAT?
OH I WAS JUST HAVING FUN.
I was a kid in a candy shop, getting to try out all sorts of new animal characters.

MY MOM JUST CALLED...
JOHNSON

MY UNCLE MILTON DIED.
OH, DALE, THAT'S *TERRIBLE*. I'M *SO SORRY*.

HE LEFT ME HIS PET STORE.
WELL THAT SURE BEATS THE *SNOT* OUT OF THE RARE MOLD COLLECTION YOUR UNCLE WALTER LEFT YOU.
This head design, short of one more eye change, is FINALLY the one I settled on. For the most part, it's the way I still draw Dale to this day.

HELLO, WILL... UH... AH' MEAN... *SIR*.
STOP PUSHIN'!
GET OFF!

OH MY LORD!
MY NAME IS ANGU... UH... *USTUS*. THAT'S RIGHT... *ANGUSTUS*.
YOU'RE ON MY LEG!
MOVE OVER!

ANGUS, WHAT ARE YOU DOING?
WE'RE TRYING TO FOOL THE NEW OWNER INTO THINKING SOMEONE STILL OWNS THE SHOP! *WERE YOU FOOLED?*

TOTALLY.
HA! SEE I TOLD YOU GUYS THIS WOULD WORK.
OKAY, SERIOUSLY... WHO JUST CUT ONE?

WELL, THIS IS THE PLACE. I'LL JUST UNLOCK THE DOOR AND...
PET STORE
CLICK! CLICK!
CLICK!

WHAT THE?
CLOSED
WHAT'S WRONG?
CLICK!
CLICK! CLICK!

THE LOCK KEEPS RE-LOCKING ITSELF...
YOU SURE YOU'RE DOING IT RIGHT?
CLICK!

THIS WAS THE BEST IDEA EVER.
HOW LONG DO YOU THINK IT WILL BE BEFORE THEY GIVE UP?
CLICK! CLICK!
PHONE BOOK

THE DOOR STILL WON'T OPEN. MAYBE WE SHOULD JUST GO HOME.
GO HOME? C'MON, JUST PUT YOUR *SHOULDER* INTO IT!

ANGUS, I CAN'T BELIEVE YOU. NOW THE NEW SHOP OWNERS HAVE PROBABLY GONE HOME. WORSE YET, YOU COULD HAVE BEEN...
PHONE BOOK

WHAM!
AAAAHHHHH!!!!

HURT.
TWITCH TWITCH
THAT'S THE SPIRIT, DUDE!

HI THERE, WE'RE THE NEW SHOP OWNERS.
WE PLAN TO TAKE *GREAT* CARE OF YOU!

OF COURSE SHOULD THE STORE EVER START TO *TANK*, WE'LL SELL TO THE HIGHEST BIDDER, WHO WILL PROBABLY USE YOU FOR *HORRIFIC LAB TESTS*. SO LET'S ALL PUT THE CUTE FACES ON WHEN CUSTOMERS ARE IN THE STORE, OKAY?

I THOUGHT YOU SAID THAT WOULD GET A *LAUGH*.
I DIDN'T KNOW GOLDFISH COULD FAINT.

While drawing the animals was always fun, drawing all of their homes quickly became a real pain.

OUR OWN PET STORE! THIS IS NEAT!
THIS IS A LOT OF RESPONSIBILITY.
JOHNSON

WHAT RESPONSIBILITY? YOU SEE AN ANIMAL, YOU TOSS IT SOME... UH... SOME...

SAY WHAT EXACTLY DO YOU GUYS EAT AROUND HERE?
I JUST MADE A PB&J. WHY? DID YOU WANT IN ON SOME OF THIS?

WHY IS THERE A SANDWICH FLOATING IN OUR TANK?
I'M GONNA' GO NUKE A HOT POCKET.

WHY HELLO, LITTLE GUPPIES.
HEY! WHO YOU CALLIN' LITTLE?
GUPPIES 1.00 EA
JOHNSON

WAIT, I JUST...
WHY DON'T YOU STICK A FINGER IN DIS TANK AND SAY DAT AGAIN, MAC?
GUPPIES 1.00 EA

FORGET IT.
YEAH... YOU'D BETTER KEEP WALKING, BUB!
GUPPIES 1.00 EA

WHY HELLO, LITTLE GUPPIES.
THAT'S IT! MEL, HOLD ME BACK!
HE AIN'T WORTH IT FRANKIE!
GUPPIES 1.00 EA

The mafia guppies are still some of my favorite characters to work with.

HI, SID.
WHAT'S WITH THE GUPPIES?
JOHNSON

WHAT ABOUT EM'?
OH NOTHING REALLY, THEY JUST THREATENED TO BURY MY HEAD IN CENTRAL PARK.
FLEM SODA

OH THAT... THEY'VE BEEN WATCHING THE SOPRANOS.
WAIT... I THINK THEY'RE LOOKING AT US.
FLEM SODA

I'M TELLIN' YA'... DAT DOG'S A SNITCH. TONIGHT HE SLEEPS WITH DA' FISHES.
I DON'T THINK THERE'S ROOM IN OUR TANK, FRANKIE
GUPPIES 1.00 EA

Flem Soda sued for using a can of their soda in this strip. Turns out they're very anti-guppy.

A LITTLE HELP HERE?
SID, WHY ARE YOU IN THE GUPPY TANK?

I TOOK A NAP, AND WHEN I WOKE UP, I HAD CONCRETE ON MY FEET.
I THINK THE GUPPIES PUT A HIT OUT ON ME.

DO THEY REALIZE YOUR HEAD IS ABOVE WATER?
I DIDN'T HAVE THE HEART TO TELL THEM.
HEY WISE GUY, MIND YOUR BUSINESS OR YOU'RE NEXT. CAPISCE?
GUPPIES 1.00 EA

HEY, SID, HOW WAS YOUR SWIM?
HA HA. VERY FUNNY.

YOU WANT I SHOULD MAKE THOSE MEAN OL' GUPPIES DISAPPEAR?
THAT WON'T BE NECESSARY.

REALLY? WHY?
WE'VE COME TO AN UNDER-STANDING.

OH DON'T TELL ME...
YES, I'M PAYING A SCHOOL OF GUPPIES FOR PROTECTION!! LET'S TRY AND KEEP FROM RUBBING IT IN, SHALL WE!?!

SO YOU THINK YOU'VE GOT THE BEST OF ME, DO YOU?

YOU THINK I'LL JUST WALK ON BY AND STUFF MY FACE RATHER THAN TAKE YOU ON. THAT'S WHAT YOU THINK ISN'T IT?

STUPID WHEEL.

WILLY, I TALKED TO ANGUS.
LUCKY YOU.

HE'S FEELING SOME ANXIETY OVER HIS WHEEL.
OH LORD.

SO I ENROLLED HIM IN A SUPPORT GROUP.
YOU'RE KIDDING, RIGHT?

HELLO, MY NAME IS ANGUS, AND I TOO FEAR THE "WHEEL OF DEATH" AS BROTHER MILTON THERE REFERRED TO IT.
HELLO ANGUS!

THEN I SEE DOUG ON THE WHEEL, ONLY SOMETHING'S NOT RIGHT... THE WHEEL IS PICKING UP SPEED...

...ALL OF A SUDDEN THAT SUCKER SHOOTS DOUG 20 FEET IN THE AIR, SCREAMING ALL THE WAY, AND HE LANDS RIGHT IN THE BOA CONSTRICTOR'S TANK.

I STILL HEAR HIS SCREAMS IN MY NIGHTMARES!

HOW IS THIS SUPPOSED TO HELP OVERCOME OUR FEAR OF WHEELS AGAIN?
IN MY NIGHTMARES!

SO YOU CAN SEE BROTHER RANDY IS DOING JUST FINE ON THE WHEEL.
JOHNSON

WHOAH! GUYS?!? IT WON'T SLOW DOWN! HOW DO I STOP IT?!?!
HE'S JUST KIDDING FOLKS... LET'S GRAB LUNCH.

FEAR THE WHEEEELLLLLL!!!
FOOM!

THIS HAS GOT TO BE THE WORST SUPPORT GROUP EVER.
HE'S ACTUALLY PICKING UP SPEED.

HOW'S THE SUPPORT GROUP GOING?
I QUIT.
JOHNSON

AFTER WHAT I SAW, I'M JUST TOO WORRIED TO SET THAT BIG WHEEL IN MOTION... I'M SCARED I'LL NEVER GET IT STOPPED.

THAT'S A FEAR WE ALL FACE.
REALLY?

WELL METAPHORICALLY SPEAKING, OF COURSE.
YEAH? HAS YOUR METAPHORICAL WHEEL EVER FLUNG A GERBIL INTO A WALL AT 90 MPH?!?! BECAUSE MINE HAS.

FIRST DAY ON THE JOB. SELLING PETS... THAT'S ME.
WE GOT MONKEYS!
JOHNSON

HELLO SIR OR MADAM, WE HAVE A LOVELY GERBIL FOR YOU TODAY... OR HOW ABOUT A PARROT... OR...

HOLD THE PHONE, ICE CREAM CONE... I DON'T WANT TO SELL ANGUS... OR WILLY... OR ANY OF MY NEW FAMILY.
WE GOT MONKEYS!

I'D LIKE TO BUY A FROG.
NOT TODAY, HOMEWRECKER! BEAT IT!
WE GOT MONKEYS!

This is why I could never work in a pet shop either.

DALE, FOR THE LAST TIME, I AM NOT HIDING ANY ANIMALS IN HERE. NOW CAN I PLEASE GET SOME PRIVACY?!?
PAPER PAL
SOAP
DUDE! THE FISH WE HID IN THE TOILET ARE FREAKIN'!
GET US OUT OF HERE!!!
I'VE BEEN BURIED ALIVE!!!
STAY AWAY FROM THE LIGHT!

SID, WE RUN A PET STORE NOW, AND WE **MUST** SELL PETS TO PEOPLE.

I KNOW YOU'VE BECOME ATTACHED TO THESE GUYS, BUT IF WE DON'T SELL SOME OF THEM, **WE'LL LOSE THEM ALL**.

LOVE WAS WHEN I LOVED YOU, ONE TRUE TIME I HOLD TO, IN MY LIFE WE'LL ALWAYS GO ON...
OH, **REAL** FUNNY.

ANGUS, WHAT HAVE I TOLD YOU ABOUT PLAYING "TITANIC" IN THE FISH TANKS?
TYTANIC
NEAR, FAAAAAR, WHEREEEVER YOU ARE, I BELIEVE THAT THE HEART DOES GO OOOON!

I JUST **HATE** THE IDEA OF SELLING THESE ANIMALS.
THAT'S LIFE SOMETIMES...
DALE

THINGS ENTER OUR LIVES, WE GROW ATTACHED TO THEM, AND THEN IN WHAT SEEMS TO BE THE BLINK OF AN EYE... **THEY'RE GONE.**
FFSSH!
SODA

LIKE YOUR LEATHER PANTS?
MAN, I **LOVED** THOSE THINGS... WHY DID THEY HAVE TO CHAFE LIKE THAT?
SODA
DALE

My constant Dale head swapping really is some kind of sickness. I don't even remember why I swapped back to this one, but it didn't last long.

SO WE HAVE TO SELL YOU GUYS TO KEEP THE SHOP IN BUSINESS.

WHY DON'T **YOU** JUST BUY US ALL? THAT WAY THE STORE MAKES MONEY **AND** WE GET TO STAY!
POIT!

MY GOD, THAT'S BRILLIANT...
EAT YOUR HEART OUT, TRUMP.

HEY, SID!
BAXTER! WHAT ARE YOU DOING HERE?

I JUST SWUNG BY TO SEE HOW THINGS ARE GOING WITH THE NEW SHOP.

WELL, OUR GERBIL JUST SWALLOWED A GOLF BALL BY MISTAKE, WE HAVE SMALL FIRE IN THE BATHROOM, AND WORD ON THE STREET IS THE GUPPIES HAVE A HIT OUT ON ONE OF OUR TURTLES.

WOW... BETTER THAN I EXPECTED.

I decided to bring Baxter by for a visit now and then. He's one of the few voices of reason in this universe.

DO YOU HAVE ANY ***TARANTULAS?*** I'D LIKE TO GET ONE FOR MY DAD.
SURE!

IS HE INTO SPIDERS?
I THINK SO... I'M GOING TO SNEAK INTO HIS ROOM AND PUT IT ON HIS CHEST ON FATHER'S DAY MORNING...
JOHNSON

THEN I'LL SCREAM "***SURPRISE!!!***"

BOY IS HE GOING TO BE EXCITED!
NO CHARGE FOR THE SPIDER IF YOU VIDEOTAPE IT.

I liked the joke, but felt the drawings lacked some punch. So I swapped out the last panel to the version below.

DO YOU HAVE ANY ***TURANTULAS?*** I'D LIKE TO GET ONE FOR MY DAD.
SURE!

IS HE INTO SPIDERS?
I THINK SO... I'M GOING TO SNEAK INTO HIS ROOM AND PUT IT ON HIS CHEST ON FATHER'S DAY MORNING...
JOHNSON

THEN I'LL SCREAM "***SURPRISE!!!***"

BOY IS HE GOING TO BE EXCITED!
NO CHARGE FOR THE SPIDER IF YOU VIDEOTAPE IT.

MAN, IT IS HOT TODAY.
TELL ME ABOUT IT. I'LL GET US SOME LEMONADE.
PET SHOP

OH HI, ANGUS. JUST NEED SOME ICE CUBES.
SURE!
FUDGE BLAST POPSICLES

THIS HITS THE SPOT!
WHY DO MY ICE CUBES HAVE LITTLE HAIRS ALL OVER THEM?
PET SHOP
JOHNSON

WHAT AISLE IS YOUR ***BUTTER*** ON?
WE DON'T CARRY BUTTER.
SODA!

LINSEED OIL?
I'M SORRY, NO.

MOTOR OIL, AXLE GREASE, MARGARINE?
NO, NO, AND ***NO.***
SODA!

SO WHAT DO YOU NORMALLY DO IN A CASE LIKE THIS?
FAINT.
SODA!
SNAILS MAKE GREAT PETS!
JOHNSON

The logo on the customer's shirt is for the band "Monotone Pictures," that features my life-long friend, Steve, on drums.

LOOK, WILLY, I GOT YOU A MIRROR.
FOR WHAT?
JOHNSON

FOR WHAT? YOU BIRDS LOVE MIRRORS.

SEE WITH YOUR SMALL BRAINS, YOU TEND TO THINK IT'S ANOTHER BIRD.
THAT'S RIDICULOUS.

I TOLD YOU HE WOULDN'T LIKE IT.
THAT'S A NICE LOOKING BIRD YOUR FRIEND HAS.

HOTCHICK MAKE UP
MAKE-UP KIT
JOHNSON

HA! HA! HA! HA!

CAN'T A GUY EVEN TAKE A NAP AROUND HERE?!?
THAT'LL TEACH YOU NOT TO SLEEP ON THE JOB, MADONNA.
I WAS GOING FOR BRITNEY SPEARS.

MY FORTUNE SAYS, "YOU'RE ON THE PATH TO SUCCESS."
"EAT MORE CHINESE FOOD." HA! THAT ONE NEVER GETS OLD!
THE CHINA GUY
JOHNSON

MINE'S BLANK.
OH THAT'S BAD... THAT MEANS YOU'RE GONNA' DIE!
THE CHINA GUY

DIE?!? BUT I'VE NEVER EVEN SKIED THE FRENCH ALPS! I'M TOO YOUNG TO DIE!

ANGUS, YOU'RE READING THE WRONG SIDE.
OH... SO I AM. LET'S SEE HERE... "YOU'RE GONNA' DIE."
WHAT DO YOU SUPPOSE THAT MEANS?
THE CHINA GUY

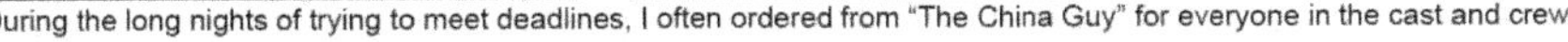
During the long nights of trying to meet deadlines, I often ordered from "The China Guy" for everyone in the cast and crew.

I'M TAKING ANGUS TO THE PARK, WILLY, YOU WANNA' COME?
UM... NO.
JOHNSON

WE'RE GOING TO EAT PIGEONS COVERED IN RELISH, AND FEED THE DOGS AND...

HANG ON... IS THAT RIGHT? THAT SOUNDS AWFUL.

IT'S HIS FIRST TIME.
SERIOUSLY, LET'S JUST EAT BEFORE WE GO.

I really liked the dynamic that Sid and Angus created. It sort of shifted Sid into the Dale role, and in turn gave him another layer.

THANKS A LOT FOR BRINGING ME TO THE PARK, SID! I HEAR IT'S...
OH WOW...
YEAH...
JOHNSON

WELCOME TO MY AQUARIUM.

I remember this strip taking me a LONG time to draw and ink.

SO YOU FLIP YOUR COIN INTO THE FOUNTAIN AND MAKE A WISH.
WHY?

WELL THEY SAY THAT IF YOU DO, AND YOUR WISH IS FOR SOMETHING YOU REALLY WANT, IT WILL COME TRUE!
REALLY?
JOHNSON

SO MAKE SURE YOU WISH FOR THE ONE THING THAT WOULD MAKE YOU HAPPIEST.

PING!

PING!

MY WISH WAS THAT I NEVER GET SOLD AND I GET TO STAY WITH YOU AND DALE FOREVER. WHAT ABOUT YOU?

WELL... UH... IT INVOLVED A TRUCK FULL OF TWINKIES AND PARIS HILTON... OKAY LOOK, I'M JUST GOING TO GO FISH MY COIN OUT AND TRY AGAIN.

Sometimes we learn the most while teaching others. It's why I try to never teach anyone anything.

AND NOW DOG COMPLEX PRESENTS SID AND ANGUS IN:
"THINGS YOU NEVER WANT TO SAY TO A HOTDOG VENDOR."

DID YOU EVEN WASH YOUR HANDS?
HOT DOGS - HOT DO
JOHNSON

TUNE IN TOMORROW WHEN SID AND ANGUS WILL BRING US:
"THINGS YOU NEVER WANT TO SAY TO A JACKHAMMER OPERATOR."

FAT CHANCE, BUTTHEAD!!!

I HOPE YOU ENJOYED THE PARK, ANGUS.

ANGUS?
NAME'S RODNEY.

WHERE'S ANGUS?
WHO'S ANGUS?

HEY, GUYS! I'M FROM THE CITY!
WELL THERE GOES THE NEIGHBORHOOD.

Even with an entire pet shop full of animals at my disposal, I still had to branch out.

YOU GUYS REALLY LIVE IN A *TREE*? MAN... I THOUGHT IT WAS JUST AN *URBAN MYTH*.
JOHNSON

WE LIVE THE WAY NATURE INTENDED US TO. WE WILL NOT BE *SLAVES* TO TECHNOLOGY LIKE YOU CITY DWELLERS.

WHAT ABOUT THE SATELLITE DISH?
OH COME ON MAN, WE'RE NOT *SAVAGES*.

SID AND ANGUS SURE HAVE BEEN GONE A *LONG* TIME.
I KNOW... DON'T REMIND ME.

FEELING A BIT *NERVOUS?*

YEAH.
JOHNSON

LIKE PUTTING SID IN CHARGE OF ANGUS WASN'T SUCH A GOOD IDEA?
YEAH.

REMEMBER THAT TIME SID ACCIDENTALLY STAPLED HIS *FACE* TO THE *FLOOR*?
I'M CALLING THE POLICE.

SID! THERE YOU ARE. I STOPPED BY THE PET SHOP, AND DALE'S *FREAKING OUT*.

HE'S ALL CONCERNED THAT HE SHOULDN'T HAVE LEFT YOU IN CHARGE OF ANGUS.
JOHNSON

OF COURSE I TOLD HIM THERE IS NO WAY YOU'D LET ANYTHING... HAPPEN... TO... UH, SID, WHO'S *THAT* IN YOUR BACKPACK?

I'M RODNEY!
I'M DEAD.
I'M LEAVING.

SO WHAT DO YOU FELLAS *EAT?*
WE LIVE OFF THE LAND.
JOHNSON

WOW! JUST LIKE THAT CROCODILE HUNTER GUY!

LOOK WHAT I SCORED FROM THE TRASHCAN TODAY! WHO WANTS IN ON A HALF-EATEN *LEMON PIE?*

OKAY, *ALMOST* LIKE THAT CROCODILE HUNTER GUY.
HEY! NICE WORK, KENNY!
THANKS. THE NEW GUY GETS THE PIECE WITH THE CIGARETTE BUTT ON IT.

OKAY... WHERE WAS THE LAST PLACE YOU SAW ANGUS?
HE WAS IN MY BACKPACK.

AND WHERE WAS *THAT?*
ON MY BACK, OF COURSE.

I MEAN WHERE WERE YOU?
I WAS HERE IN THE PARK.

HE'S NOT EVEN TRYING.
BAXTER, ARE YOU EVEN TRYING?
I'M TRYING NOT TO STRANGLE YOU... DOES THAT COUNT?

HELLO, SHERIFF'S DEPARTMENT? MY DOG IS MISSING.

DON'T FORGET *ANGUS.*
OH YEAH... AND HE HAS A GERBIL IN HIS BACKPACK.

YES, *I KNOW* DOGS DON'T NORMALLY WEAR BACKPACKS OR HANG OUT WITH GERBILS.

LET ME TRY.
NO, *YOU'RE* THE NUTJOB, *PAL!* HANG ON... MY PARROT HAS SOMETHING HE WANTS TO SAY TO YOU.

BOY, THIS IS *GREAT!* EATING TRASHCAN PIE, LIVING IN THE TREE... *AWESOME!*
JOHNSON

IT'S NOT WORKING OUT... WE'D LIKE YOU TO LEAVE.
PARDON?

LOOK... IT'S NOT YOU. IT'S US.
WE CAN WORK THIS OUT... PLEASE GIVE ME ANOTHER CHANCE.

HE STILL WON'T LEAVE.
GIVE HIM THE OL' "THERE ARE PLENTY OF OTHER SQUIRRELS IN THE PARK" LINE.
MY EX USED THAT ONE ON ME.

I'VE LOST ANGUS... MAN, THIS IS SO BAD.
HEY, SID.
TRACY GREEN.COM
LONGSHOT
LIQUID! YEAH

SWEET BETTY WHITE! *ANGUS!* WHERE HAVE YOU BEEN?!?
HANGING WITH SOME SQUIRRELS, BUT I GOT BORED WITH THAT SCENE, SO I SPLIT.
LIQUID! YEAH

YOU GET KICKED OUT?
TOTALLY. I'VE NEVER FELT LIKE SUCH AN IDIOT.
LIQUID! YEAH

I ONCE ATE AN ENTIRE *FOOTSTOOL* BECAUSE I THOUGHT IT WAS A GIANT PIECE OF *CANDY*.
THANKS, SID, THAT REALLY HELPS.

Tracy Green wrote the foreward to this book. It turns out he also walks around scratching his website into park benches. Longshot was the name of the band I played in for 10 years.

DALE'S GONNA' BE *STEAMED*... WE'RE REALLY LATE!
CAN WE STOP FOR A SNACK?

ANGUS, WHAT DID I *JUST* SAY?
I KNOW, BUT ALL I HAD WAS A BIT OF LEMON PIE...
JOHNSON

I'M SORRY, ANGUS... THERE JUST ISN'T TIME.
HEY, CHECK IT OUT! *CARAMEL APPLES!*

TRY THIS BAD BOY... IT HAS MARSHMALLOWS ON IT!
I GOT MINE STUCK TO MY HEAD.

I'M GOING OUT TO LOOK FOR SID.
ZZZZ... *SNORT!*
JOHNSON

HI, DALE.
SID! ANGUS! OH THANK HEAVEN. WHERE HAVE YOU BEEN?
PLEASE DON'T BE MAD.

I'LL EXPLAIN THINGS TOMORROW. WE'RE PRETTY TIRED, SO WE'RE GOING TO BED.

I'M SUPPOSED TO BE MAD, BUT I CAN'T STOP SMILING.
YEAH... *REAL* TOUCHING. WAS THAT A CARAMEL APPLE?

HI FOLKS! I'D LIKE TO TALK TO YOU THIS MORNING ABOUT DALE.
COME AGAIN?

MORE SPECIFICALLY HIS *HEAD*.
HANG ON... *WHAT?*

THAT THING HAS CHANGED SHAPE MORE TIMES THAN A *WARM LUMP OF CLAY*.
I DON'T LIKE WHERE THIS IS GOING.
JOHNSON

LET'S TAKE A WALK DOWN MEMORY LANE, STARTING WITH THIS *HIGHSCHOOL PHOTO*.
SHUT THE *#@$!%* CAMERA *OFF*.

At this point, I knew how ridiculous my head swapping had become, so I decided to have some fun with it.

WELCOME BACK! I BROUGHT SOME PHOTOS TO AID US ON OUR "MANY HEADS OF DALE FLEMING TOUR!"
JOHNSON

HERE IS A SHOT OF DALE FROM EPISODE 52.

AND HERE IS A SHOT OF MY NOSE AND ONE OF A MISSHAPEN BALLOON.
YOU DOCTORED THOSE.

HERE'S ONE OF A LARGE SQUASH.
EVER HEAR OF OL' YELLER?

OUR "HEADS OF DALE FLEMING TOUR" CONTINUES WITH THIS SHOT FROM WHAT I LIKE TO CALL DALE'S "JOHN TESH PHASE."
FUNK & GONE

SID?!? OPEN THIS DOOR! YOU'RE GIVING THAT STUPID HEAD TOUR AREN'T YOU?
JOHNSON

I AM NOT... I WAS JUST TRIMMING... UH... STUFF.
SORRY... I THOUGHT I HEARD SOMETHING ABOUT JOHN TESH.
BRRRRR...

I BET JOHN TESH'S DOG NEVER HAS TO LOCK HIMSELF IN THE BATHROOM.
I HEARD THAT!!!

THIS NEXT DALE HEAD IS ONE I CALL THE OL' "HATCHET CHIN."
THAT'S IT! TOUR'S OVER.
JOHNSON

NO IT ISN'T.
IT IS, OR I WALK. I DON'T HAVE TO PUT UP WITH THIS.

OH, HE'S BLUFFING. WHO WANTS TO SEE DALE'S OLD CHIN SLICE THIS BREAD?
GET MY AGENT ON THE PHONE.

MAYBE I SHOULD STOP. ANYBODY ELSE SEE THAT VEIN ON HIS FOREHEAD? I COULD ACTUALLY HEAR THAT SUCKER THROBBING.

WHILE THE AUTHOR WORKS OUT SOME ISSUES OVER THE CURRENT STORYLINE WITH ONE OF THE ACTORS, SID THE DOG HAS GRACIOUSLY OFFERED TO DRAW TODAY'S DOG COMPLEX STRIP.
ENJOY.

HELLO MY NAME IS DALE! LOOK AT MY STRANGE HEAD!
THAT'S OKAY I STILL LOVE YOU.
FINGER
CHICKEN
BUFF

SID YOU ARE PERFECT. WOULD YOU LIKE A STEAK?
I'D RATHER GIVE IT TO THE HOMELESS.
WEIRD HED
STEAK
BY: SID

MY HEAD IS DUMB!
I DONATED MY SPLEEN TO CHARITY!
BAT
ICE CREAM

Folks always like it when Sid draws a strip. In fact, I think they'd be just fine with it if they drew them all.

WE HAVE A *SPECIAL FRIEND* DROPPING BY THE PET SHOP TODAY, SO YOU TWO BE ON YOUR *BEST* BEHAVIOR.
FUZZY THING
JOHNSON

DALE ALWAYS ACTS LIKE WE'RE SO IRRESPONSIBLE.
TOTALLY.

THIS IS BORING. WANNA' TRY GLUING OURSELVES TO THE CEILING?
TOTALLY!

I like that Angus is destroying Sid at their game of checkers.

A KID IS STOPPING BY?
HIS NAME IS ALDO.
Squeaky Toys
GOOD
BAD

HIS DAD BOUGHT THE OLD RESTAURANT NEXT DOOR, AND THE APARTMENT ABOVE IT.
SQUEAK
SQUEAK
Squeaky Toys
GOOD
BAD

DALE, I DON'T *DO WELL* AROUND KIDS. THEY FREAK ME OUT.
YOU'LL BE FINE.
Squeaky Toys
GOOD
BAD

HAVE YOU SEEN HOW SMALL THEIR HANDS ARE, DALE? *IT'S NOT RIGHT!*
DUDE, YOU'RE MOLTING IN MY SQUEAKY TOYS.
Squeaky Toys
GOOD

A few years later, I would work with a guy who had the exact same fear of kid hands. His feathers hardly ever fell out though.

HI, I'M ALDO. ARE YOU SID?
WHAT? UH *NO*... I'M BAXTER.
CHUNKY SOUP
JOHNSON

DO YOU KNOW WHERE I MIGHT FIND DALE?
SURE. FOLLOW ME.
CHUNKY SOUP

DO YOU WORK HERE AT THE PET SHOP?
HECK NO... I JUST LIKE TO HANG OUT AND WATCH STUFF BLOW UP.

STUFF BLOWS UP?
OH *SURE*... OR BREAKS... OR MELTS... OR RUNS BY *ON FIRE* AND *SCREAMING*.
CHUNKY SOUP

I MEAN IT, SID... NO MORE GLUING YOURSELF TO THINGS.
HI, MR. FLEMING.

OH HEY, ALDO. I DIDN'T SEE YOU COME IN. THIS IS SID.
HEY I KNOW YOU!
FUZZY THING

YOU'RE THE KID THAT BOUGHT THE TARANTULA TO SURPRISE YOUR DAD WITH FOR FATHER'S DAY!
JOHNSON

HOW DID THAT GO?
THE PARAMEDIC THAT REVIVED HIM SAID NEXT YEAR I SHOULD PROBABLY GO WITH SOCKS.

SO WHAT BRINGS YOU TO TOWN, ALDO?
MY DAD BOUGHT THE RESTAURANT NEXT DOOR. WE OPEN IN A WEEK.
CHUNKY SOUP

NEAT! WHAT KIND OF FOOD?
MOSTLY ITALIAN.
CHUNKY SOUP

AH... WELL TELL HIM I SURE AM LACTOSE INTOLERANT!
COME AGAIN?
CHUNKY SOUP

LACTOSE INTOLERANT... IT'S ITALIAN FOR EXCITED... I THINK.
WOW, I TOTALLY THOUGHT MR. FLEMING WAS JOKING WHEN HE SAID YOU SAY THINGS LIKE THAT.
CHUNKY SOUP

THESE HERE ARE LOVEBIRDS.
THERE'S ONLY ONE.
CHUNKY SOUP

GINA, WHERE IS ANDY?
I KICKED HIM OUT.
CHUNKY SOUP
JOHNSON

BUT LOVEBIRDS MATE FOR LIFE.
YEAH? TELL THAT TO HIM AND THAT TRAMP OF A COCKATIEL I CAUGHT HIM WITH.

NOTHING IN OUR SHOP REALLY FOLLOWS NATURE'S ORDER.
YOU WANNA' SEE LOVE, TRAMP? COME ON OVER... I'D LOVE TO KNOCK THOSE FEATHERS OFF YOUR FACE!
HUNKY SOUP

ANGEL SEED, ARE YOU MAD?
DON'T TRY THAT ANGEL SEED CRAP WITH ME.
LOVEBIRDS CHEAP

BUT, FEATHERBUNS, THAT COCKATIEL MEANT NOTHING.
YOU REPULSE ME. I'M GOING TO SLEEP.
LOVEBIRDS CHEAP

LOVEBIRDS CHEAP

CAN WE AT LEAST CUDDLE?
TRY IT, AND YOU'RE GOING TO WIND UP CUDDLING WITH THE BUSINESS END OF THE GARBAGE DISPOSAL.
LOVEBIRDS CHEAP
JOHNSON

ALDO, THIS IS ANGUS.
HEY GUYS!
OAT BLAST

SO... UH... WHAT ARE YOU DOING?
I'M TAKING A MUDBATH!
OAT BLAST

IN MAPLE AND BROWN SUGAR OATMEAL?
THEY SAY IT'S GREAT FOR THE OL' PORES.

I THINK THEY MEAN PLAIN OATMEAL.
I'M NOT SO SURE THAT HE CARES.
CHECK IT OUT! I'M A MUD MONSTER WITH GREEN THINGEES FOR EYES!!!
OAT BLAST
JOHNSON

WILLY, THIS IS ALDO.
CHUNK SOUP

NICE TO MEET YOU.
OKAY... WAIT... SLOW DOWN! YOU'RE MOVING TOO FAST!! SMALL HANDS... SMALL HANDS!
DING DING DING
FOOM!
CHUNK SOUP

IT'S NOT YOU... HE FLASH MOLTS AROUND YOUNG PEOPLE.
OH COME ON! THE KID TOTALLY CHARGED ME!

INK

INK

INK

INK

What? You don't have a framed photo of a shoe in your house?

DID ALDO TAKE OFF?
YEAH, HE LEFT AFTER WILLY BLEW UP.
WHEAT BLOBS

DID HE HAVE A GOOD TIME?
I THINK SO.
WHEAT BLOBS

I HOPE YOU GUYS DIDN'T FREAK HIM OUT.
ARE YOU KIDDING? HOW COULD WE FREAK HIM OUT?
WILLY SHAVED ME.
WHEAT BLOBS

OKAY, WE MAY HAVE FREAKED HIM OUT A LITTLE.
HOLY CRAP! I HAVE NIPPLES!!
WHEAT BLOBS

I GOT A LETTER!
WHO'S IT FROM?

I DON'T KNOW... THERE'S NO RETURN ADDRESS.
MAYBE IT'S FROM A HOT BABE!
TRASH

NAH... LETTERS FROM HOT BABES ALWAYS SMELL LIKE PERFUME.

THIS ONE SORT OF SMELLS LIKE CABBAGE AND TUNA.
SNORT SNORT
THE PERFUME COUNTER MUST HAVE BEEN HAVING A SALE.

Sorry about the image quality on this one. For whatever reason the master file wouldn't open. Stupid computers.

SO OPEN YOUR LETTER.
HECK NO! IT'S PROBABLY BAD NEWS!
JOHNSON

OH THAT'S SILLY. IT'S PROBABLY GOOD NEWS.
YEAH?!? WHAT IF IT'S THE WORST NEWS WE'VE EVER HEARD?

YOU WANNA' BURY IT?
I'LL GET THE SHOVEL.

SO DID WE GET ANY MAIL?
I GOT A LETTER.
JOHNSON

WHAT DID IT SAY?
NO IDEA. I BURIED IT IN THE PARK.

YOU WHAT?
IT WAS TOO MUCH PRESSURE. WHAT'S INSIDE? IS IT BAD? IS IT GOOD? I COULDN'T TAKE IT, SO I BURIED IT. I'M GONNA' GO SNAG A COOKIE.

HUH... I WONDER IF THAT WOULD WORK WITH THE CABLE BILL.

PSSST... HEY KID, WANNA MAKE A BUCK?
I'M KIND OF BUSY... MAYBE SOME OTHER TIME.
GUPPIES 1.00 EA
HUG A CRAB!
Monkey Food

IT'S REAL EASY... JUST DELIVER A MESSAGE FOR ME.
THAT'S ALL?
GUPPIES 1.00 EA
MONKEY

I'LL MAKE IT WORTH YOUR WHILE.
OKAY, SURE... WHY NOT.
HUG A CRAB!

THE GUPPY CRIME BOSS, MR. GUPINO, SAYS YOU HAVE DISHONORED HIS FAMILY. HE SENT YOU THIS.
THE HEAD OF THE LITTLE PLASTIC DIVER FROM THEIR AQUARIUM?
JOHNSON

THAT GUPPY CRIME BOSS IS PRETTY ANGRY WITH YOU.
WHAT THE HECK DID I DO?
PLASTIC DIVER HEAD
FORBES

YOU KNOW, I'M NOT SURE. HANG ON... I'LL GO ASK.
OH YOU DO THAT, SALLY.
JOHNSON

MR. GUPINO SAYS YOU ATE A DEAR FRIEND OF HIS FOR LUNCH YESTERDAY.
I HAD FISHSTICKS!

ADOPT A
BEAVER TODAY!
SQUEAKY TOYS
FISHERMAN'S FRIEND TARTAR SAUCE
GREAT FOR FISH!
NEW SMELL!
12% LESS LUMPS!
INDIVIDUAL JARS-36 COUNT
YOU'RE NEXT! LOVE, DALE
I DON'T TINK DIS GUY IS TAKIN' US SERIOUSLY, FRANKIE.
GUPPIES $1.00 EA
FLEAS MAKE
GREAT PETS
JOHNSON

Did you know that fleas make great pets?

DOG COMPLEX

BY: DAVE JOHNSON

FLOUR

EGGS
FLOUR

FLOUR
COOKIES

PLOOSH!
FLOUR

SPLOIT!!
COOKIES

COOKIES

MR. GUPINO, HAVE YOU WORKED THINGS OUT WITH DALE?
OH DAT'S ALL BEEN *TAKEN CARE OF*.
JOHNSON

ROCKO HERE DID SOME *WORK* ON DAT *SAUSAGE BRAIN'S* CAR.
YEAH, YEAH... SOME *WORK*. GOOD ONE, BOSS.

WHAT KIND OF *WORK*?
BRAKE WORK, IF YA' KNOW WHAT I'M SAYIN'.

OH MY LORD! DALE JUST LEFT IN THE CAR TO GET US DINNER!
YOU MAY WANNA' TINK ABOUT ORDERING A PIZZA, KID.
EXTRA ANCHOVIES.

HE DRIVES A WHITE CAR WITH FOUR WHEELS AND A WINDSHIELD. MODEL? OH NO, OFFICER... DALE'S NICE LOOKING, BUT HE'S NO MODEL. OH THE CAR? I'M NOT SURE... DID I MENTION IT'S WHITE?
JOHNSON

WHO WANTS PIZZA?!?
SWEET BETTY WHITE! YOU'RE OKAY!

UH YEAH... I'M FINE.
THE GUPPIES SAID THEY MESSED WITH THE BRAKES ON YOUR CAR.

WELL THAT EXPLAINS WHY OUR NEIGHBOR, MRS. STEAMBLAT, PASSED ME ON THE HILL DOING 90.
AT LEAST SHE WON'T BE LATE FOR BINGO TONIGHT.

SEE YOU PUT THE TATER TOTS RIGHT ON THE JELLY AND...
SID! ANGUS! GUESS WHAT?

IT FINALLY HAPPENED!
JOAN RIVER'S FACE IMPLODED ON ITSELF?
YOU GOT A DATE?
JOHNSON

WE'RE GETTING A MONKEY!
OH WOW!

I FEEL LIKE A KID ON CHRIST-MAS MORNING OPENING THE BEST PRESENT EVER!
YOUR PARENTS GIFT-WRAPPED A MONKEY?
BOY, THAT SUCKER MUST HAVE STUNK.
This was the start of a storyline that introduced one of the most beloved characters in the "Dog Complex" cast.

WHY THE GRIN?
I ORDERED US A MONKEY!

SO?
SO? SO!?! WORD GETS OUT AND CUSTOMERS WILL START POURING IN TO SEE IT!

YES I CAN HEAR IT NOW, "YOU KNOW WHAT? THAT MONKEY REMINDS ME... I COULD REALLY USE A BRAIN DEAD GERBIL."
JOHNSON

"REALLY? I'VE BEEN LOOKING FOR A GUPPY THAT THINKS IT'S A MOB BOSS. GOOD THING I CAME TO SEE THAT MONKEY."
MONKEY ENVY.

OUR MONKEY IS BEING DELIVERED TODAY!
WHAT IF IT'S A MEAN MONKEY?

MONKEYS AREN'T MEAN, ANGUS.
YEAH? YOU EVER SEEN ONE OF THOSE WILDLIFE DOCUMENTARIES WHERE A MONKEY TAKES DOWN A LAME GAZELLE?
JOHNSON

THOSE ARE CHEETAHS.
SO WE'RE GOING TO HAVE AN ANIMAL IN OUR STORE THAT CAN EAT A CHEETAH? FORGIVE ME FOR NOT BEING MORE EXCITED.
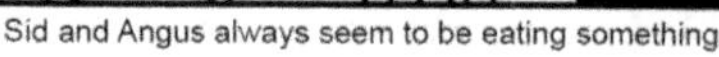
Sid and Angus always seem to be eating something.

OUR MONKEY JUST ARRIVED! COME HELP ME OPEN THE CRATE!
NEAT!

WOW! THE CRATE'S HUGE!
I'LL START PULLING NAILS. YOU READ THE CARE SHEET.
LIVE ANIMAL
HANDLE WITH CARE!

WE'LL NEED TO BUY HIM SOME SMOKES.
SID, THAT'S TERRIBLE. WHERE WOULD YOU GET AN IDEA LIKE THAT?
JOHNSON

TIP #8: "MONKEY ONLY SMOKES FILTERED CIGARETTES." IT'S RIGHT UNDER "BOOZE PREFERENCE."
LET ME SEE THAT LIST.

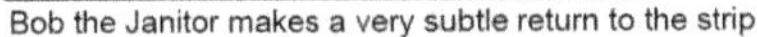
Bob the Janitor makes a very subtle return to the strip.

LAST NAIL. GET READY TO BE MONKEYSIZED!
PING!
THAT SOUNDS PAINFUL.
JOHNSON

TA... DA?

BOY, AM I GLAD TO BE OUT OF THAT CRATE. SOMEONE ORDER A MONKEY?
COME AGAIN?
MONKEY

ORDERING A MONKEY OFF THE INTERNET MAY NOT HAVE BEEN MY BEST IDEA.
MAYBE YOU MISSED THE SHIRT.

I figured the Monkey gag would be a 6-8 strip story line. Little did I know that he would still be living with Dale and Sid to this day.

LISTEN, PAL, I ORDERED A MONKEY, AND YOU SENT ME A MAN... A REALLY HAIRY MAN.

IS THAT SO? WELL YOU SURE SEEMED TO BE SELLING MONKEYS LAST WEEK.

OH REALLY? OH REALLY?!? WELL THAT'S JUST FINE. MAYBE I'LL JUST DO THAT!

WHAT DID HE SAY?
HE SAID I SHOULD DOUBLE CHECK THE NUMBER, BECAUSE THEY DON'T SELL MONKEYS OR HAIRY MEN AT THE SHADY GROVE RETIREMENT CENTER.
JOHNSON

YOU ARE NOT A MONKEY.
YES I AM.
MONKEY

IT'LL TAKE MORE THAN A SHIRT TO CONVINCE ME.
ONE SEC.

OOO OOO... UH... EEE EEE.
MONKEY

SID, FOR THE LAST TIME HE IS NOT A MONKEY.
I'M JUST SAYING HIS BANANA EATING IS VERY CONVINCING!
JOHNSON

DID OUR MONKEY SHOW UP YET?
YEAH... HE'S PRETTY NEAT.
CHOCO SYRUP YUM!

HEY WHAT IS THIS, A NUNNERY OR SOMETHING? THERE AIN'T A SINGLE BREW IN THE FRIDGE. I'M RUNNING TO 7-ELEVEN FOR SOME NACHOS AND A SIXER.
CHOCO SYRUP YUM!
JOHNSON

WOW... I'VE NEVER SEEN ONE THAT CLOSE UP BEFORE. HE'S PRETTY BREATHTAKING.
PLUMBER'S CRACK AND ALL, HE TRULY IS A MARVEL OF NATURE.
CHOCO SYRUP YUM!

Tell me that chocolate syrup on cheese puffs doesn't sound awesome.

OH HEY! I HEAR YOUR INTERNET MONKEY SHOWED UP.
DON'T START, WILLY.

WHAT? THAT MONKEY IS GOING TO DRAW IN LOTS OF NEW CUSTOMERS!

AND?

AND IF THAT BOMBS, WE HANG A SOCK FROM SOME GUY'S NOSE AND TELL EVERYONE WE HAVE ELEPHANTS FOR SALE!
OH HARDEE HAR.

OKAY, MONKEY BOY, THIS CHARADE ENDS NOW.
FINE, BUT I'D STILL LIKE TO STAY.
MONKEY

I'M HANDY WITH TOOLS AND I'LL ONLY EAT AS MUCH AS A MONKEY WOULD. PLUS YOUR DOG LIKES ME. THAT HAS TO BE WORTH SOMETHING.
BEER
MONKEY

DALE, ANGUS AND I WANT TO PLAY SMOKEY AND THE BANDIT. WHERE DO WE KEEP THE FAKE MUSTACHES?
BEER
MONKEY

DID I MENTION I'M HANDY WITH TOOLS?
OH... AND I'LL NEED THE KEYS TO YOUR CAR.
BEER
MONKEY

I liked how Sid just sort of accepted Monkey into his world almost instantly. It's odd for me to say, since I wrote the scripts, but Sid always kind of wrote for himself in a way.

HI. I NEED TO TALK TO YOU ALL ABOUT SOMETHING.
JOHNSON

WHAT IN THE #@$% IS GOING ON WITH MY HEAD? IT LOOKS LIKE I HAVE A CASHEW TRYING TO BURROW OUT OF MY SKULL.
MONKEY

IT'S SO DEFORMED...
UH... MONKEY, WE JUST DID MISSHAPEN HEAD JOKES TWO MONTHS AGO.
MONKEY

AH CRAP... I HAD SOME REAL KNEE SLAPPERS.
WE'VE GOT AN OVERSIZED NOSE STORYLINE IN ABOUT 3 WEEKS. I'LL PENCIL YOU IN.

THANKS AGAIN FOR LETTING ME STAY, MR. FLEMING.
SURE, I COULD USE THE HELP.
MONKEY

CAN WE KEEP THE OTHER THING BETWEEN US?
WHAT, THAT YOU'RE NOT A MONKEY?

YEAH. THE OTHERS REALLY SEEM TO ACCEPT ME. I'D HATE TO MESS THAT UP.

YES, REJECTION FROM A GERBIL CAN BE A TOUGH THING.

OKAY WHEN YOU PUT IT LIKE THAT, IT SOUNDS WEIRD.
YOU'RE GOING TO FIT RIGHT IN AROUND HERE.
MONKEY

DOG COMPLEX
BY DAVE JOHNSON

$20 or best offer

LOOK AT WHAT ANGUS AND I FOUND AT A YARD SALE TODAY!
A LAWN-MOWER?

AIN'T SHE A BEAUT?
SHE WAS ONLY 20 BUCKS!
SID, WE LIVE IN THE CITY. WE DON'T NEED A LAWN-MOWER.

WELL SURE, WE DON'T NEED ONE FOR LAWN MOWING, BUT THINK OF ALL THE OTHER STUFF IT CAN DO!
LIKE?

WELL... WE CAN USE IT TO SLICE SAUSAGE... OR... CHOP SALAD! AND THOSE DOCUMENTS YOU NEEDED SHREDDED THE OTHER DAY? MOW EM'!

AND SAY GOODBYE TO THE BARBER!
HE'S RIGHT! WE'LL JUST MOW IT!
YOU'RE TAKING IT BACK.

BUT I'M TOTALLY JONESING FOR A LAWN-MOWER SALAD NOW.
IS THAT A CARPET SNAG I SEE? LET'S MOW IT!
I FEEL LIKE I'VE JUST STEPPED INTO THE INFOMERCIAL FROM HELL.

YO' MONKEY! WHAT'S SHAKIN'?
I'M WATCHING FOOTBALL.

COOL! CAN I WATCH WITH YOU?
IT AIN'T MY COUCH.

YOU'D THINK THEY COULD SEE BETTER WITHOUT THE HELMETS.
NOT A BIG FOOTBALL FAN, ARE YOU?

SEE, I DON'T GET THIS...
WHAT NOW?
BREW

WELL THE IDEA IS THAT THE GUY WITH THE *FOOTBALL* NEEDS TO STAY ON HIS *FEET*, RIGHT?

YET THEY GIVE THE BALL TO THE *SMALLEST* GUY ON THE FIELD, RATHER THAN ONE OF THOSE *HUGE* ONES.

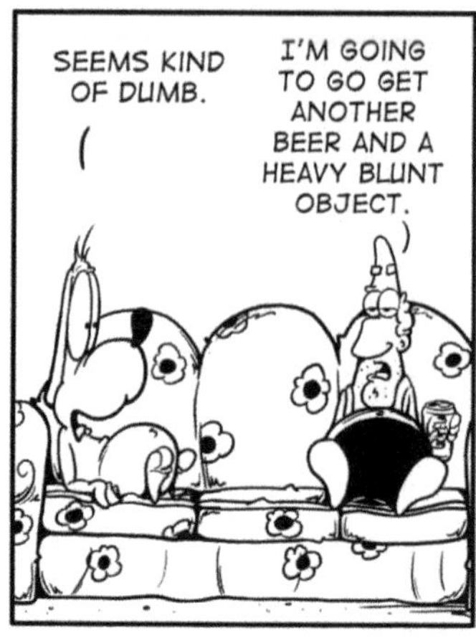
SEEMS KIND OF DUMB.
I'M GOING TO GO GET ANOTHER BEER AND A HEAVY BLUNT OBJECT.

This is another example of Sid being a reflection of my wife at times.

SO... YOU'RE WATCHING FOOTBALL WITH SID.
UH... YEAH.
SODA

HOW'S *THAT* WORKING OUT?
IT COULD BE BETTER.

LIKE IF HE WASN'T IN THE ROOM?
LIKE IF HE WAS CHAINED TO A *BUICK* AND DRIVEN OFF A *CLIFF*.
MONKEY

The "LS" on the fridge stands for "Longshot," but for the life of me I can't remember what the "HNA" stands for.

SEE THE GUY WITH THE BALL HAS TO TRY AND GET ACROSS THAT LINE.
THEY SHOULD GIVE IT TO ONE OF THE BIG GUYS.

I AGREE. OKAY, NOW THAT THEY'VE SCORED, THEY KICK THE *P.A.T.*
WHAT'S *THAT* STAND FOR?

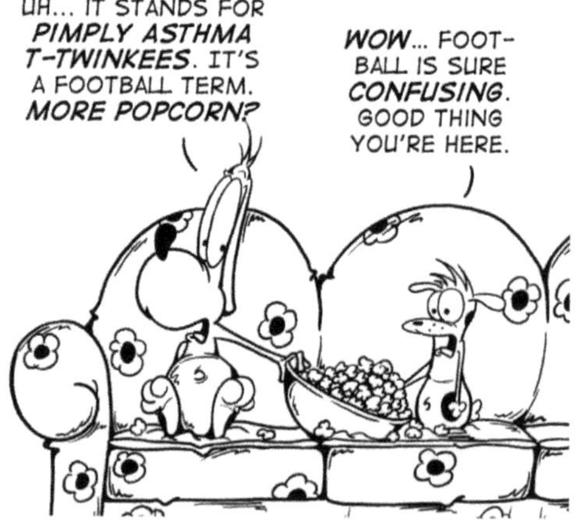
UH... IT STANDS FOR *PIMPLY ASTHMA T-TWINKEES*. IT'S A FOOTBALL TERM. *MORE POPCORN?*
WOW... FOOT-BALL IS SURE *CONFUSING*. GOOD THING YOU'RE HERE.

THE BEER ON THAT AD CLAIMED TO BE THE *COLDEST TASTING* BEER.

BUT HOW CAN SOMETHING *TASTE COLD?* COLD DOESN'T TASTE LIKE *ANYTHING*, DOES IT?
I HAVE NO IDEA.

DON'T YOU SEE? IT'S LIKE SAYING, *"WOW!* THIS IS THE *LOUDEST TASTING* SODA *EVER!"*
OH YEAH... *I GET IT!*

PASS ME SOME MORE PEANUTS! I LOVE THAT *ROUND TASTE!*
OKAY, I WAS WRONG. I'M STILL *TOTALLY* LOST.

This one got me a few nice emails. It's also another example of me not being the guy you want pick horses, as I rarely called the ones that were going to get me such emails.

HEY THERE YOU ARE, MONKEY! THANKS FOR LETTING US WATCH **FOOTBALL** WITH YOU!
IT **WON'T** HAPPEN AGAIN.
BEER
MONKEY
JOHNSON

WELL.... WE'RE OFF TO GO TOSS THE **OL' PIGSKIN** AROUND.
IT'S NOT REALLY A FOOTBALL... **IT'S A SHOE!**
SWEET.
BEER
MONKEY

WHY ARE SID AND ANGUS WEARING **COOKWARE** AND THROWING A **SHOE** AROUND IN THE STREET?
YOU NEED TO STOP ASKING SO MANY QUESTIONS AND JUST ENJOY THE **SILENCE**.
BEER

DOG COMPLEX
BY: DAVE JOHNSON!

GROCERY BARN

HEY! I USED TO **LOVE** THESE THINGS WHEN I WAS A KID.
YOU KNOW ... I VE GOT EXTRA QUARTERS.
25¢

OH WHAT THE HECK. **FIRE HER UP!!**
YOU GOT IT, **MAJOR TOM!**
I THOUGHT HIS NAME WAS **MONKEY**.

PREPARE FOR **LIFTOFF!**
25¢

THIS IS **GREAT!**
I WANNA TRY!
ME TOO!
WHIR! WHIR! WHIR!

I THINK THEY OVERCHARGED ME FOR THE **ASPARAGUS** AGAIN, IT ... UH WHAT IN THE **HECK** ARE YOU GUYS DOING?
WHIR! WHIR!
WHIR!

WE RE RELIVING OUR CHILDHOOD!!
COME ON, DALE, **HOP ON IN!**
OH... I THINK I M A BIT TOO **OLD**.
GROCERY BARN

THEY VE BEEN ON IT FOR OVER AN HOUR.
I'M CALLING THE COPS.

DALE, CAN WE TURN THE SHOP INTO A **HAUNTED HOUSE** FOR HALLOWEEN THIS YEAR?
JOHNSON

OH SID... I DON'T HAVE TIME.
DON'T WORRY... ANGUS AND I WILL TAKE CARE OF THE **WHOLE THING**.

THE TWO OF YOU... **WITHOUT** SUPERVISION... YEAH... **NOT** GONNA' HAPPEN.
OH GOOD... SO YOU **WILL** HELP THEN. **THANKS, DALE!**
FUZZ THING

SURE! I'LL JUST... **HEY!!** THAT'S **NOT** WHAT I SAID!
FUZZ THING

OKAY, THE FIRST THING WE NEED TO DO IS COME UP WITH THE THEME FOR OUR HAUNTED HOUSE.
BALLERINAS!!!
JOHNSON

NO, NO, NO ... WE NEED SOMETHING SCARY.
HOW ABOUT "SID AND ANGUS CHAINSAW HOUSE OF DEATH!"

BINGO! I'LL GO ASK DALE IF WE CAN USE CHAINSAWS!

HE SAID ELECTRIC PENCIL SHARPENERS ARE OUR LIMIT.
MAN... WE'RE GONNA NEED LOTS OF EXTENSION CORDS.

MONKEY! COME QUICK! ANGUS HAS BEEN IN A HORRIBLE ACCIDENT!!!
MONKEY
JOHNSON

OH MY LORD!!!
OH THE HUMANITY! RIGHT THROUGH THE OL' MEAT GRINDER!

I'LL GO GET HELP! YOU GET SOME TUPPERWARE AND SCOOP HIM UP! AND FOR THE LOVE OF PETE, STAY AWAY FROM THE BBQ!!!

THIS ONE IS A DEFINITE KEEPER FOR THE HAUNTED HOUSE.
I'M GOING TO SMELL LIKE MEAT FOR WEEKS.

If I were forced to pick a favorite strip, it would probably be this one. I've just always had a soft spot in my heart for meat.

YOU'RE BACK! DID YOU PICK UP THE INFLATABLE DRACULA?
THEY WERE SOLD OUT.

AW MAN! DID YOU AT LEAST GET A GOOD REPLACEMENT LIKE FRANKENSTEIN OR THE WOLFMAN?
I GOT THIS.
LIFE SIZE!

"LIFE-SIZE INFLATABLE MARTHA STEWART"
LOOK, I KNOW YOU WANTED A ...
SUPER SCARY!

HEY, ANGUS!!! WE'RE GONNA SCARE THE PANTS OFF SOME KIDS WITH THIS SUCKER!
AND HERE I WAS WORRIED HE MIGHT NOT LIKE IT.
LIFE-SIZE
JOHNSON

HILLTOP MAXIMUM SECURITY HOME FOR THE CRIMINALLY INSANE
EWARE!
KEEP OUT!
DRINK MILK!

HEY WALT, EVERYTHING IN ORDER?
HE'S GONE... SLAUGHTERHOUSE STEVE HAS ESCAPED!!

THINK WE SHOULD TELL SOMEONE?
IT'S ALREADY TOO LATE!
JOHNSON

WE EVEN HAVE RUBBER SPIDERS! COULD THIS HAUNTED HOUSE BE ANY SCARIER?
HILLTOP
TO BE CONTINUED ...

This could have been Crazy Karl, or Butcher Brad, but I went with Slaughterhouse Steve, after my good friend of the same name. Well... at least the "Steve" part.

OH HEY, DALE! I DIDN'T SEE YOU STANDING THERE.
WOW!!! KILLER COSTUME!

IT S AWESOME! NOW, LET'S HEAR YOUR BEST PSYCHOTIC AXE WIELDING KILLER VOICE!
YOU'RE ALL GOING TO DIE.
HILLTOP

OKAY, WE NEED TO WORK ON THE VOICE ... THAT WAS TERRIBLE.
AT LEAST HE SMELLS BAD!
HILLTOP
JOHNSON

DOG COMPLEX
BY: DAVE JOHNSON!

YOU VE REALLY OUTDONE YOURSELF, SID.

OH, AREN'T WE JUST TICKLED PINK WITH OURSELVES?
YOU CAN TALK?!?

YEAH... AND I GOT A BONE TO PICK WITH YOU, PAL.
WHAT DID I DO?

WHAT DID YOU DO? YOU SCOOPED OUT MY HEAD CHEESE AND REPLACED IT WITH A CANDLE!!!
WELL YEAH, I GUESS I DID DO THAT.

BUT IT'S TRADITION.

TRADITION? TRADITION?!? COME HERE, PAL. LET'S START A NEW TRADITION!
GET AWAY FROM ME!!!

BUT YOU LOOK SO NICE AND RIPE! LET ME CARVE SOMETHING INTO YOUR HEAD!!!
GET AWAY!!!

DO I EVEN WANNA' KNOW?
NEXT YEAR WE'RE SKIPPING HALLOWEEN.
MONKEY
BEER

AGAIN, TO CONFIRM OUR TOP STORY... SLAUGHTERHOUSE STEVE, THE CONVICTED KILLER HAS ESCAPED FROM PRISON.
BEER
JOHNSON

THAT'S PRETTY CRAZY STUFF.
YEAH... BUT WHAT'S THE CHANCE OF HIM PICKING A PET SHOP TO TERRORIZE?
CH 4 NEWS

ONE OTHER NOTE... ALL OF HIS PREVIOUS VICTIMS WERE PET SHOP EMPLOYEES.
CH 4 NEWS
DEATH

WELL I DIDN T SEE THAT ONE COMING.
MAYBE I'LL GO CHECK ON SID.
CH 4 NEWS

I TOLD DALE WHAT TO DO ONCE THE KIDS GET HERE.
CANDY CORN
JOHNSON

HAVE YOU NOTICED THAT HE'S ACTING KINDA **WEIRD**?
YEAH ... IS THAT A REAL **AXE**?
CANDY CORN

THONK!!!
CANDY CORN

LOOKS REAL TO ME.
HEY, DALE! YOU DROPPED YOUR AXE!!!
CANDY CORN

MONKEY, I CAN'T FIND SID OR ANGUS **ANYWHERE**!
RING!!!

HELLO?
MR. FLEMING? THIS IS THE HILLTOP MAXIMUM SECURITY HOME FOR THE CRIMINALLY INSANE. WE THINK ONE OF OUR ESCAPED INMATES MAY BE HEADED YOUR WAY.
JOHNSON

HOLD ON ... YOU HAVE MORE THAN ONE ESCAPED INMATE?
OH **YES**. WE TEND TO LEAVE THE CELLS **UNLOCKED** AROUND THIS TIME OF YEAR ... MAKES FOR A BETTER HALLOWEEN.

THANKS TO YOU, MY DOG AND GERBIL ARE PROBABLY **DEAD**, BUCKO!
THERE MAY BE HOPE...
JOHNSON

PAL, THOSE TWO AND A GUY WHO PRETENDS TO BE A MONKEY ARE MY **ONLY** FRIENDS. I'LL TAKE ANYTHING YOU CAN GIVE ME.
BEER
MONKEY

LEGEND SAYS THAT STEVE SPARES THOSE WHO ARE "**PURE OF HEART** IN AN ALMOST **NAIVE** WAY." DOES THIS DESCRIBE YOUR TWO PETS?
BBRAAAHHH!!!

THEY'RE REALLY MORE OF A "NAIVE IN A MAKE-YOU-WANNA'-HANG-YOURSELF WAY." IS THAT CLOSE ENOUGH?
MONKEY

CHECK IT OUT! **I M FRANKENSTEIN**!
SID! **YOU'RE OKAY**! I WAS WORRIED YOU WERE TRAPPED WITH **CRAZED KILLER**!

OH HE TOOK OFF... SAID SOMETHING ABOUT US BEING "PURE."
GOOD THING... IMAGINE IF HE HAD FOUND MONKEY ...

FOR THE LAST TIME, KID... THE **HAUNTED HOUSE** IS DOWNSTAIRS. **NOW BEAT IT**. UNCLE MONKEY WANTS TO WATCH **GIRLS GONE WILD**.
BEER
JOHNSON

Sid was the virgin who made it out of the horror movie alive. Monkey was the pot-smoking, porn-watching, Heathen. They hardly ever do.

I SURE AM GLAD YOU TWO ARE SAFE.
THAT MAKES THREE OF US!

MONKEY AND I WERE SO WORRIED ABOUT YOU TWO. WE JUST ... SAY ... HAS ANYONE SEEN MONKEY?
BLEH!
BLEH!
BLEH!

ARE WE OUT OF BAND-AIDS OR WHAT?
I'LL GO GET THE BACTINE.
MONKEY
BEER
JOHNSON

ANGUS! THERE YOU ARE! I COULDN'T FIND ANYONE FOR THE LONGEST TIME.

YOU WANT A HIT OF MY PB N J?
SURE, BUDDY!

POIT!
JOHNSON

WE'RE OUT OF JELLY AGAIN, SO I USED MAYO.
TANGY, YET NUTTY...

After the Halloween story arc, I took a month-long break to recharge. To make up for this, I had some of the characters "find" each other again.

SO WE FEED THE SAUSAGE THROUGH THE FAN WITH CHEESE AND SOME MAYO AND... BOOM! INSTANT SANDWICHES!!!
MAYO

COOL!!!
I KNOW!!!
JONSON

SID... ANGUS... WHERE IN THE HECK HAVE YOU BEEN? I'VE BEEN LOOKING ALL...
BEER
MONKEY

BWAH!
GET THE BREAD! THAT SUCKER WORKED LIKE A CHARM!
I'M SO GLAD I FOUND YOU TWO.

MILK!

MORNIN' FELLAS!!!
MILK!
JOHNSON

MILK!

SID... TELL ME ANGUS JUST WALKED BY DRESSED AS A CIGARETTE...
EITHER THAT OR SOMEONE SLIPPED SOME PCP INTO OUR SPECIAL K.
MILK!

I have no idea where I got the idea for this next storyline, but I'm almost positive it had nothing to do with PCP.

START OVER.
I TOLD YOU... I WAS AT THE MALL, AND A GUY CAME UP TO ME.
JOHNSON

GO ON...
HE SAID THAT HIS CIGARETTE COMPANY WAS LOOKING FOR A **MASCOT**.

THEN I SAID I DIDN'T SMOKE, AND THAT I WAS PRETTY SURE IT ISN'T HEALTHY.

YET HE **STILL** TALKED YOU INTO IT?
SOMEWHERE BETWEEN THE CORNDOG, THE ORANGE JULIUS, AND THE TALK OF MY OWN ASHTRAY, I GUESS I GOT CAUGHT UP IN THE MOMENT.

ANGUS, DON'T YOU SEE WHAT THEY'RE DOING HERE?
NOPE.

BIG TOBACCO IS USING **YOU** TO APPEAL TO **KIDS**.
COME AGAIN?

THEY'RE USING YOUR **CUTENESS** TO CONVINCE CHILDREN TO SMOKE!
OH THAT'S JUST **SILLY**.

ANGUS, THEY NAMED YOU PUFFY MCFUNTIMES!!!
LISTEN... YOU NEED TO RELAX. HERE... HAVE ONE OF THESE CANDY CIGARETTES. THEY'RE **CHERRY FLAVORED!**
JOHNSON

SID, WHY DID ANGUS JUST LEAVE HERE DRESSED AS A **CIGARETTE**?
GROCERY
SODA
JOHNSON

HE GOT A JOB AS A CIGARETTE COMPANY MASCOT. SAID SOMETHING ABOUT A RIBBON CUTTING CEREMONY AT A TOYS-R-US.
GROCERY
SODA

COME TO THINK OF IT, MAYBE I SHOULD GO GET HIM.
YES... MAYBE YOU SHOULD.
GROCERY

HAVE YOU SEEN ANGUS CIGARETTE COSTUME?
YEAH... IT'S **ALL** I CAN THINK ABOUT.
MONKEY

FOR FIFTEEN YEARS I SMOKED THREE PACKS A DAY. I QUIT, AND NOW HAVE THE MOTHER OF ALL CIGARETTES LIVING WITH ME.
1994
1986
1979
ZIPPO

WELL YEAH, BUT IT'S NOT LIKE YOU CAN **SMOKE** HIM OR ANYTHING.
JOHNSON

MONKEY? YOU DO KNOW YOU CAN'T **SMOKE** ANGUS, **RIGHT**?
HE'S GOT A **FILTER** AND EVERYTHING.

HI! I'M PUFFY MCFUNTIMES! WOULD YOU LIKE TO TRY A CIGARETTE?
UH... THOSE ARE BAD FOR YOU.

ONE MOMENT PLEASE.

"SCENARIO 7: Subject questions health benefits of smoking."
KIDS ARE SMOKERS TOO
A GUIDE TO SELLING SMOKES

IT SAYS I M SUPPOSED TO PUT YOU THROUGH A WOOD CHIPPER.
UM... I THINK I HEAR MY MOM CALLING ME.
KIDS ARE SMOKERS TOO

TODAY IS APRIL 25TH, WHICH HAPPENS TO BE THE ARTIST S **BIRTHDAY**.

HE'S 30...

TO MAKE HIMSELF FEEL BETTER, HE HAS DECIDED TO LIST **ALL** OF THE THINGS HE KNOWS ARE STILL **OLDER** THAN HE IS.

THE GREAT WALL OF CHINA.

KATHIE LEE GIFFORD.

SEE YOU NEXT WEEK.
(APOLOGIES TO CHINA)

I don't remember taking my 30th Birthday that hard, so I think I really just wanted to get out of drawing the strip for a day. And take a cheap shot at Kathie Lee.

DALE, I WENT AND GOT ANGUS LIKE YOU ASKED.
GOOD... NOW KEEP HIM AWAY FROM MONKEY.
FAST GRO!

WHY?
LET S JUST SAY MONKEY SHOULD NOT BE AROUND A GIANT WALKING CIGARETTE.
FAST GRO!

SO I SAID, "HEY KID, IF PEOPLE DIE FROM SMOKING, HOW COME JOHN WAYNE IS STILL ALIVE?"
PUFFY? WILL YOU MARRY ME?
MONKEY
BEER

WILLY, HAVE YOU SEEN ANGUS?
NO... WHY?

HE'S DRESSED AS A GIANT CIGARETTE AND I'M AFRAID MONKEY MIGHT TRY SOMETHING CRAZY.
OH, DALE... LIKE MONKEY WOULD EVER TRY ANYTHING.
FISH

HE TRIED TO SMOKE ME!
ONE SMALL TASTE OF YOUR SWEETNESS, PUFFY, THAT'S ALL I'M ASKIN'!!!
SOMEONE GET A TRANQUILIZER OR A MARLBORO OR SOMETHING!!!

FUN WITH
PUFFY MCFUNTIMES
A-MAZE-ING!!!
HELP PUFFY GET TO THE MAN WHO IS OUT OF SMOKES!
COLOR THE HAPPY LUNGS!!!
WORD JUMBLE!!!
USE THE LETTERS BELOW TO ANSWER THE QUESTION!
WHAT DOES PUFFY ALWAYS SAY?
________ _____!
M K S G N I O U E S L R
ANSWER - SMOKING RULES!
WORD SEARCH!!!
CAN YOU FIND ALL OF THE GREAT WORDS IN THE PUZZLE BELOW?
GREAT
FUN
HIP
TASTEY
FILTER
PACK
LIGHT
MENTHOL
COOLER
MACHO
L F M D H F U N
G R E A T I M Q
R V N X A L A L
P Y T W S T C I
A Z H K T E H G
C O O L E R O H
K Q L S Y X N T
H I P C A N R E
DID YOU KNOW?
MORE PEOPLE DIED LAST YEAR FROM LIGHTNING, SHARK ATTACKS, CAR ACCIDENTS, PLANE CRASHES, ELECTRIC SHOCK, GUNSHOT WOUNDS, PIT FIGHTING, STABBINGS, AND DRIVE BY SHOOTINGS COMBINED THAN FROM SMOKING?!?!
REMEMBER, KIDS... SMOKING IS BAD FOR YOU.

FOR THE LAST TIME, ANGUS, I'M **REAL** SORRY ABOUT BREAKING YOUR CIGARETTE COSTUME.

LOOK... IS THERE **ANYTHING** I CAN DO TO MAKE IT UP TO YOU?
MONKEY

MONKEY

HARK, DAMSEL IN DISTRESS, I AM BREWMAN AND THIS IS MY SIDEKICK **BEERGUT**.
IT'S BEER**NUT**, AND I SAID WITH **FEELING**!!!

RING!!!
RING!!

RING!!
CLICK!
2:13AM

UH... HELLO?

WHAT!?! IS SHE OKAY? I'LL BE ON THE **FIRST PLANE** I CAN FIND... TELL HER I'M ON MY WAY.
TO BE CONTINUED...

I always hated when I was forced to write a joke-less strip, but in this case, I felt it was warranted.

MONKEY, WAKE UP.
ZZZZ... **SNORT**! BUT KATIE... WHAT IF TOM FINDS OUT?

MONKEY!
HUH... WHA... **DALE**? I WASN'T TALKING IN MY SLEEP WAS I?

MONKEY, MY **MOM** IS IN THE **HOSPITAL**. I'M FLYING OUT TO SEE HER, AND I M LEAVING YOU **IN CHARGE**.
SOUNDS AWESOME... ZZZ...

GOOD GOD, IT SOUNDS EVEN **WORSE** WHEN I SAY IT OUT LOUD.
ZZZ... WHAT DO YOU MEAN IT WAS **TOM'S** IDEA?

Monkey is not dreaming about Tom Cruise and Katie Holmes, so please don't send me hate male, Scientologists. Come to think of it... don't send me any kind of mail.

I PUT SOME COFFEE IN A THERMOS FOR YOUR DRIVE TO THE **AIRPORT**.
I SURE HOPE MOM IS OKAY.

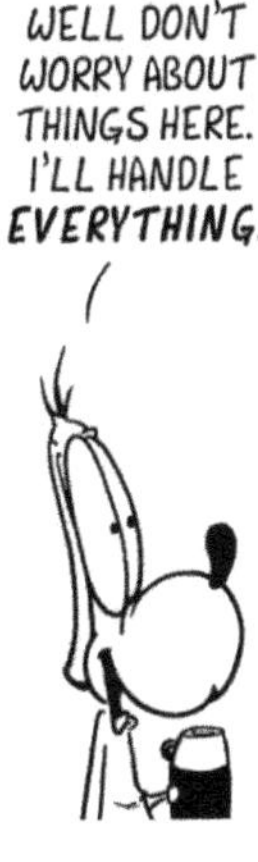
WELL DON'T WORRY ABOUT THINGS HERE. I'LL HANDLE **EVERYTHING**.

ACTUALLY, I PUT **MONKEY** IN CHARGE.

YOU REALIZE A SICK MOTHER IS THE **ONLY** THING SAVING YOU FROM A THERMOS LOAD OF HOT COFFEE DOWN YOUR UNDERPANTS, RIGHT?
UNDERSTOOD.

MORNING, SID!
PAN CAKE MIX
JOHNSON

I MADE YOU PANCAKES WITH CHOCOLATE CHIPS IN THEM, JUST HOW YOU LIKE. CAN I GET YOU SOME...

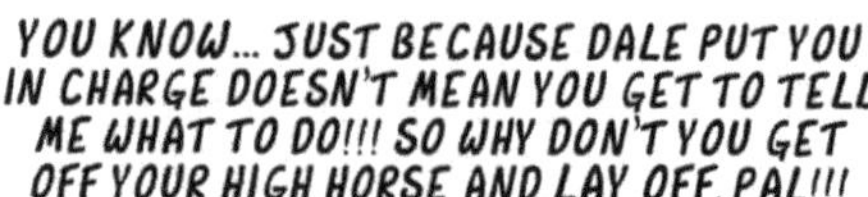
YOU KNOW... JUST BECAUSE DALE PUT YOU IN CHARGE DOESN'T MEAN YOU GET TO TELL ME WHAT TO DO!!! SO WHY DON'T YOU GET OFF YOUR HIGH HORSE AND LAY OFF, PAL!!!

...COFFEE?
I THINK SOMETHING POOPED IN OUR PANCAKE MIX.

DOC, HOW IS MY MOM?
MR. FLEMING, SIT DOWN.
DIOLOGY
JOHNSON

OH GOD, IS IT BAD?!?
SHE'S GOING TO BE FINE.

THEN WHY AM I SITTING DOWN?
DALE, YOUR MOM HAS BEEN TELLING ME YOU HAVE TROUBLE DATING. HERE'S A PICTURE OF MY DAUGHTER.

AM I BEING PUNK'D?
IGNORE THE FACIAL HAIR. I'VE GOT A COLLEAGUE WHO SWEARS HE CAN LASER IT RIGHT OFF.

HI, MOM.
OH, DALE, I'M SO GLAD YOU'RE HERE!

THE DOCTOR SAID IT WAS JUST INDIGESTION.
I THOUGHT IT WAS MY TICKER FOR SURE.

HE ALSO SAID YOU TOLD HIM I CAN'T GET A DATE.
DID HE SHOW YOU THE PICTURE OF HIS DAUGHTER?

SHE HAS A MUSTACHE, MOM. WE'RE TALKING TOM SELLECK.
YOU'D BE LUCKY TO FIND A WOMAN WHO'S HALF THE MAN TOM SELLECK IS!!!

X-ROCKET 3000
FLICK
FLICK

X-ROCKET 3000
FLICK
JOHNSON

DALE WOULDN'T HAVE CARED ABOUT SOME STUPID OL' ROCKET.
HANG ON... THAT WAS A ROCKET?

DOG COMPLEX
SODA!

HEY, ANGUS!

NOT NOW, SID, I'M ALMOST AT LEVEL TEN!
SODA!

SEE I EMBEZZLED MONEY FROM THE CORPORATION I OWNED.
SODA!

ON THE NEXT LEVEL I INVADED A COUNTRY AND SHOT IT ALL UP.

THEN I CARJACKED SOME NICE LADY AND DROVE AROUND BEFORE SMASHING INTO AN ICE CREAM TRUCK.

ON LEVEL EIGHT I BECAME A MOVIE STAR AND GOT ADDICTED TO DRUGS!
BUT YOU'RE NOT OLD ENOUGH TO BUY AN ADULT RATED GAME...

OH THE CONTROLLER ISN'T PLUGGED IN. I JUST LIKE TO PRETEND WHILE I WATCH THE NIGHTLY NEWS.
I WONDER IF HILLARY HAS HEARD ABOUT THIS...
OH YEAH... LIKE YOU DIDN'T SEE THAT ONE COMING.
SODA!

At the time, Hillary Clinton was jumping up and down on the nightly news over violent videogames.

MY MOM IS DOING WELL, SID. WE'RE BACK HOME NOW, SO I THOUGHT I'D CALL. HOW ARE THINGS GOING?
JOHNSON

YES, MONKEY IS STILL IN CHARGE. NO, HE IS NOT TRYING TO RUIN ALL OF YOUR FUN. OH, SID, STOP IT... MONKEY DOESN'T HATE ANGUS.

YOU'RE JUST MAD BECAUSE YOU AREN'T IN CHARGE.

NO... YOU ARE NOT ALLOWED TO STAGE A COUP AND OVERTHROW HIS TOTALITARIAN REGIME. NOW STOP WATCHING THE HISTORY CHANNEL AND GO OUTSIDE.

MS. FLEMING'S HOUSE... DALE SPEAKING.
DALE, IT'S MONKEY. I WANT YOU TO KNOW THAT I'VE NEVER LIKED SID OR ANGUS.

UH... WHAT'S WRONG WITH YOUR VOICE, MONKEY?
WHILE YOU'VE BEEN GONE, I'VE BEEN REALLY MEAN TO THEM. TODAY I PUNCHED SID. I ALSO THINK THAT ANGUS LOOKS LIKE A YOUNG RALPH MACCHIO.

I'M HANGING UP NOW, ANGUS.
OKAY, DALE, TALK TO YOU LATER.

I TOLD YOU NOT TO USE THE MACCHIO LINE!!!
WELL WOULD IT HURT FOR YOU TO SAY IT ONCE IN A WHILE?!?
JOHNSON

MONKEY, SID WANTS TO SEE YOU.
OH WHAT NOW?
BEER
WAR AND PEACE
JOHNSON

SID, I KNOW YOU DON'T LIKE ME BEING IN CHARGE, BUT...
MONKEY, MONKEY, MONKEY. I DON'T CARE ABOUT THAT.
MONKEY

REALLY?
NAH... IN FACT, I'VE MADE YOU LUNCH. IT'S RIGHT IN HERE.
MONKEY

YOU'D THINK I WOULD HAVE ASKED MYSELF, "HEY, MONKEY... WHY WOULD SID MAKE YOU LUNCH IN THE CLOSET?" BUT NOOOOO...

WITH MONKEY TIED UP IN THE CLOSET, WE CAN DO WHATEVER WE WANT!

LET'S GO GET A BUNCH OF JUNKFOOD AND RENT SOME PAULY SHORE MOVIES!

BUT THAT'S WAY TOO FAR TO WALK.
HMM... YOU'RE RIGHT.
JOHNSON

OKAY, ONE LAST TIME... WE LET YOU OUT TO DRIVE US TO THE STORE AND BLOCKBUSTER THEN WE TIE YOU BACK UP.
SUUUURE... JUST LET OL' UNCLE MONKEY OUT.

Blockbuster Video has since gone out of business. Yet another victim of the mighty Internet.

THANKS FOR DRIVING US TO BLOCKBUSTER, MONKEY.
I'M DRIVING YOU TO THE POUND.
JOHNSON

ESPECIALLY AFTER WE TIED YOU UP... WAIT... WHAT?
I'VE HAD IT. YOU'RE GOING TO THE POUND.

MONKEY, NO!!!
LET GO OF THE WHEEL, SID!!!
SCREEEEEEEEECCHHH!!!

WELL THIS CAN'T BE GOOD...

I don't think Monkey would have ever really driven them to the dog pound. He managed to convince Sid otherwise.

AND THEN THE CAR WENT OFF THE CLIFF.

YEAH... EVERYONE IS OKAY.

THE CAR? IT SEEMS TO BE FINE. WE'LL KNOW MORE ONCE WE GET IT OUT OF THE TREE. DALE? HELLO?

HE HUNG UP.

DOG COMPLEX PRESENTS...
HOW'D THEY DO THAT???

EMAILS HAVE BEEN POURING IN, ASKING HOW WE STAGED OUR RECENT CAR DRIVING OFF THE CLIFF STRIP. WAS IT STUNTMEN? COMPUTER ANIMATION? MAGIC?!?
MAKE-UP
CLOSED SET
JOHNSON

ACTUALLY, THE ENTIRE SET, RIGHT DOWN TO THE ACTORS, WAS MADE OUT OF MASHED POTATOES, THEN FILMED VIA STOP-MOTION! PRETTY NEAT, HUH?

WE'RE HAVING STEAK AND POTATOES FOR DINNER. I NEED THE PINTO.
HOW ABOUT MONKEY INSTEAD?
HEY!!!

I'D LIKE A REFUND ON THE FISH I BOUGHT.
WHAT'S WRONG WITH IT?
BOBBY BROWN
WE HAVE BEAVERS!
JOHNSON

I BOUGHT THE FOOD AND BOWL YOU SUGGESTED, AND IT STILL DIED.
THERE'S NO WATER IN THE BOWL.
WE HAVE BEAVERS!

WE HAVE BEAVERS!

MOM SAID I WASN'T READY FOR A PET.
THAT'S WHY SHE OWNS THE BASEMENT AND YOU LIVE IN IT.
WE HAVE BEAVERS!

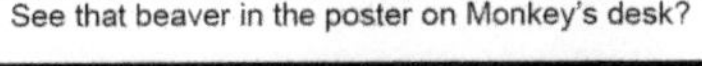
See that beaver in the poster on Monkey's desk? Keep him in mind, as he'll show up more later in the book.

WHAT THANKSGIVING DINNER IS LIKE WHEN YOU SHARE IT WITH A BIRD.

COULD YOU PLEASE PASS THE FRUIT LOOPS?
SURE. ANYONE WANT MORE TOMATO SOUP?
THIS IS RIDICULOUS.
BOY! THOSE PILGRIMS REALLY KNEW HOW TO EAT!
APPLE JACKS!
BEETS
BEER
EGGOS
TOMATO
JOHNSON

Each time you see a black box or two in a strip, it usually means I came up with the joke late, and had to crank it out as quickly as possible. Black boxes fill space well.

I JUST GAVE THE GUPPIES THEIR CHRISTMAS GIFT.
BEER
CHIA PET

I THINK THEY LL LIKE IT.
WHAT EXACTLY DO YOU GIVE A TANK FULL OF FISH WHO THINK THEY RE IN THE MOB?
BEER
CHIA PET

HOLY CHEESE CANNOLI, FRANKIE! THE SOPRANOS BOX SET!
YEAH... THE KID S ALRIGHT, JOHNNY.
GUPPIES $1.00 EA
SOPRANOS
JOHNSON

The guppies should have been featured more often. I love those little guys.

DOG COMPLEX

BY: DAVE JOHNSON

THIS EGGNOG SMELLS **FUNNY**.
WE WERE OUT OF EGGNOG. THIS IS **WOOD GLUE**!
PTTOOOY!!!
MONKEY
SO WE TIE THE **CANS** TOGETHER LIKE THIS.
ANGUS
SID
SANTA RULES!
WHEN **SANTA** TRIPS ON EM', WE LL WAKE UP. THEN WE **TACKLE** HIM, AND TAKE THE **BEST TOYS** IN HIS BAG!
NEATO!!!
LATER THAT NIGHT...
CLANK!
CLINK!
CLANK!
ANGUS! WAKE UP! I HEAR OUR **ALARM** GOING OFF! **SANTA** IS DOWNSTAIRS!
WE'LL SNEAK UP ON HIM!
CLANK!
SANTA SURE KNOWS A LOT OF **SWEAR WORDS**...
CLONK!
THERE HE IS!!! GET HIM!!!
!
CLANK!
TACKLE!
YULE LOG!
WHAM!
KRINGLE!
TONIGHT WE ALL LEARNED A VALUABLE **LESSON**.
YEAH... DON'T GO FOR A **MILLER** FROM THE FRIDGE ON CHRISTMAS EVE IN A HOUSE FULL OF **IDIOTS**.
AND GOD BLESS US EVERY ONE!

The Holiday Season is, without a doubt, my favorite time of year. In the time since this strip was written, my wife and I have produced two kids, and now I have even more reason to love it.

SID?!? WHAT IN THE **HECK** ARE YOU DOING DOWN HERE?
I'M MAKING A **TELEPORTER**!
MONKEY
PAINT
JOHNSON

MONKEY
CLANK!
TINK!

BUT YOU NEED HELP TOASTING A **POP-TART**.
IT'S OKAY... I LEARNED THIS OFF THE **INTERNET**!
MONKEY
CLINK!

WHY MAKE A **TELEPORTER**?
TO MOVE STUFF FROM ONE POD TO THE OTHER. **DUH**.
JOHNSON

WHAT WILL THAT HELP?
SAY YOU HAVE **BREAD** IN THIS POD, BUT **BOLOGNA** IN THAT ONE.
CAT

JUST **ZAP** THE BOLOGNA OVER TO THE BREAD POD, AND **VOILA**! **INSTANT SANDWICH**!

BUT THE PODS ARE **FOUR FEET APART**. WHY NOT JUST **WALK** OVER AND...
I THINK I'LL GO MAKE A SANDWICH.
CAT

THERE IS NO WAY YOUR TELEPORTER IS GOING TO WORK.

JUST HAND ME THE STICKY STUFF AND TWISTER WAND AND GO AWAY.
KNOWN TO SOME AS THE SUPERGLUE AND SCREWDRIVER.

MAN... MONKEY HAS NO FAITH IN ME. I'M NOT AN IDIOT.

THREE MINUTES LATER.
I GLUED THE TWISTER WAND TO MY FOREHEAD.
WELL COLOR ME SHOCKED.

DID YOU GUYS HEAR?!? THE SEAHAWKS WON AND ARE GOING TO THE SUPERBOWL!!!

I'VE BEEN A FAN FOR A LONG TIME, AND BELIEVE ME... I NEVER THOUGHT I'D SEE THE DAY!

WE'RE GOING TO THE SUPERBOWL!!! WOOHOOO!!! I NEED A BEER!!! HOO! HOO! HOO!

SEATTLE HAS A FOOTBALL TEAM?
MAYBE IT'S THAT ARENA LEAGUE.

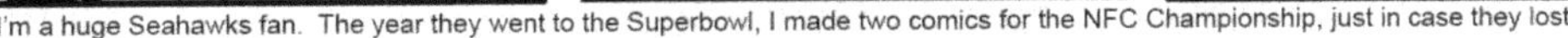
I'm a huge Seahawks fan. The year they went to the Superbowl, I made two comics for the NFC Championship, just in case they lost.

DID YOU HEAR? THE SEAHAWKS LOST AND AREN'T GOING TO THE SUPERBOWL.

I'VE BEEN A FAN FOR A LONG TIME, AND I THOUGHT THIS MIGHT FINALLY BE OUR YEAR.

THIS SUCKS. WE BETTER HAVE BEER IN THE FRIDGE OR THINGS ARE GOING TO GET UGLY.

SEATTLE HAS A FOOTBALL TEAM?
MAYBE IT S THAT ARENA LEAGUE.

SWEET BETTY WHITE! MY TELEPORTER IS FINISHED!
PAINT

OR AT LEAST I THINK IT IS... WHAT I NEED IS A TEST SUBJECT. BUT WHO?
I THINK WE ALL KNOW WHERE THIS IS GOING...

IT'S JUST MAKING MY BUTT FEEL KIND OF WARM.
I'LL CRANK THE JUICE.

THE END?

The strip you just read wasn't supposed to be the last. Sid was supposed to complete his experiment, and become a famous dog, or at very least eat another sandwich. Angus was supposed to become half gerbil, half bumble bee, or something like that. Monkey was supposed to drink more beer. Willy was supposed to get over his fear of kids.

And Dale? Well he was just going to spend his days trying to keep his head from changing again.

That never happened, and the strip abruptly ended.

Two events took place within a week of each other that resulted in the "end" of Dog Complex. The first is that Universal Press Syndicate offered me an online syndication contract. The idea was that I would get a cut of the revenue from the ads on their site, and they in turn would put my strip next to others in their stable, like "Garfield," "FoxTrot," "Calvin & Hobbes." Not only that, but if the strip did well with readers on the site, we'd talk a full syndication contract in newspapers.

The downside was that the pay was going to be very low at first, and not even close to enough to support a family on.

At the same time, the company I worked for as a contractor offered me a great paying full-time job. The downside there, was that I was going to have to work some pretty crazy 80 hour weeks from time to time.

I loved my jobs, but knew I wouldn't have enough time for both, so I had to make the tough decision to end "Dog Complex," and accept the full-time job offer with my company. I still work for that same company, and I love going to work every single day, but I always wonder what would have happened if I had gone with the syndication deal instead.

I guess we'll never know.

CHAPTER 3: GUEST STRIPS AND DANGLY BITS

The following pages contain various bonus strips that I could dig up. Some are failed "next strips" from me, such as "Happenstance," or the never-named, "Project Park." Others are guest strips that I drew for other artists, or ones that were drawn for me on weeks when I was sick or on vacation.

The most exciting part, at least for me, is that there are some new "Dog Complex" strips. Heck a couple I came up with while creating this book, and those have never even seen the light of day!

In the years since I ended "Dog Complex," I've come to realize that it really won't ever end. For me it was lightning in a bottle, and when I tried to replicate that with "Happenstance" or "Project Park," it just didn't work. Without knowing it, I created a dog that really can't be replaced in my head. Sid is a part of my life, and I've said at times that he is my dog, and Dale is a good friend of mine.

So I'll always create "Dog Complex" strips. I might find time down the road to create a strip a day again, but chances are it will be one here and there when I get a free moment or two. Visit www.3Dave.com , which is my personal site, and I will try to keep everyone updated on Sid and the gang.

HI EVERYONE! GREAT NEWS...
DAVE AND TESSA ARE EXPECTING THEIR FIRST CHILD!

IT'S DUE IN DECEMBER!
YEP... JUST IN TIME FOR CHRISTMAS!

MAN... THAT KID IS GOING TO GET HOSED ON PRESENTS EVERY YEAR.
I KNOW.

THEY REALLY SHOULD HAVE PLANNED BETTER.
MAYBE THEY HATE KIDS...
START OVER!
MONKEY

I posted this strip on my website, 3Dave.com, the day I was given the go-ahead from my wife to announce the birth of our first child.

WELL LOOK WHO'S HOME!

HOW WAS YOUR FIRST DAY ON THE JOB?
AWFUL. NOBODY RESPECTS A SECURITY OFFICER.

DID THEY GIVE YOU A GUN?
THEY GAVE ME THIS.

WHY IS YOUR PEPPER SPRAY MINT MOCHA FLAVORED?
IT'S BINACA.

I tried re-starting "Dog Complex" in 2007, and it was short-lived. It's a shame too, as this storyline could have been a lot of fun.

HOW DID MONKEY'S FIRST DAY AS SECURITY GUARD GO?
NOT GOOD.

I HAD AN UNCLE WHO WAS A SECURITY GUARD.
REALLY?

YEP, HE WAS NIGHT WATCHMAN IN HIS CAGE. ONE TIME HE FOILED A PLOT TO TIP OVER THE BIG METAL HAMSTER WHEEL.

HE WAS A WHEEL HERO.
ANYONE LAUGHS AND I'M EMAILING THEM A VIRUS.

Sorry these strips are so blurry, but a simply couldn't not find the originals. I really shouldn't be allowed out of my own home.

IT'S TIME I TEACH YOU KARATE, SO YOU CAN DEFEND YOURSELF AS A SECURITY GUARD.
YOU DON'T KNOW KARATE.

I WATCHED ALL THREE KARATE KID FILMS LAST NIGHT.
YEAH? WELL I'M NOT PAINTING ANY FENCES.

WELL THAT'S JUST SILLY. WE DON'T EVEN HAVE A FENCE.

HOWEVER, LET ME SHOW YOU UNCLOG THE TOILET
LET ME SHOW YOU PUNCH THE DIP'S BRAIN.

HI FOLKS! LAST STRIP I SAID THAT I HAD WATCHED ALL **THREE KARATE KID** FILMS.
JOHNSON

READERS WERE QUICK TO POINT OUT THAT THERE WAS ACTUALLY A **FOURTH** FILM, STARRING THE LOVELY HILLARY SWANK.

WHILE I'M SURE IT'S A FINE FILM, I'M A **MAN**, AND PREFER MY ACTION FILMS STRICTLY **MAN ON MAN**.

UH... WAIT... I MEAN... THAT CAME OUT **WRONG**!
PLEASE TELL ME WE GOT THAT ON TAPE.

MY FIRST NIGHT AS A **SECURITY GUARD**...
JOHNSON

AND THEY SAID I'D GET CREEPED OUT... **HA**!

THE ONLY THING I'M GETTING IS **THIRSTY**. I NEED A COLD ONE AND...
CRASH!
BRITNEY'S DIGNITY

...A CLEAN PAIR OF SHORTS.
BRITNEY'S DIGNITY

IT IS RAINING **CATS AND DOGS** OUT THERE!
IF I HAD A **NIPPLE** FOR EVERY TIME I'VE HEARD **THAT** EXPRESSION.

NICKLE.
PARDON?

IT'S HAD A "**NICKLE**," NOT "NIPPLE."
I DON'T THINK SO.
JOHNSON

WELL I **KNOW** SO.
LET'S JUST AGREE TO DIP A BEE.

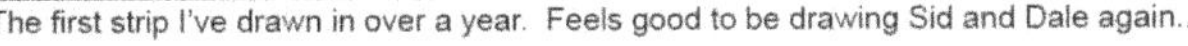
The first strip I've drawn in over a year. Feels good to be drawing Sid and Dale again...

I CAN'T BELIEVE OUR TICKETS WERE **$30** BUCKS.
I CAN'T BELIEVE WE'RE ABOUT TO SEE "**FAST CARS AND FASTER BULLETS**" IN **3D**!
JOHNSON

THE SNACKS WERE ANOTHER **$15**.
THE STUNTS WERE ALL PERFORMED BY **JACKIE CHAN'S** HALF-BROTHER!
SHOOT STUFF
COMING SOON!
POP CORN

I'M GOING TO BE OUT **A HUNDRED BUCKS**!
HE'S GOING TO TAKE OUT AN ENTIRE **SCHOOLBUS FULL OF NINJAS**!
POP CORN

WE SHOULD HAVE **STAYED HOME**.
WE SHOULD DO THIS **MORE OFTEN**!
POP CORN

HAPPENSTANCE
THE COMIC

"Happenstance" was a comic I started not long after I put "Dog Complex" on hiatus. The idea being that I would draw one strip every two weeks. I only made it through 6 strips before I stopped.

HAPPENSTANCE

HEY, ROY, **HAPPY BIRTHDAY**!

YOU KNOW I HATE BIRTHDAYS, BERNIE.

BUT I GOT YOU A **GIFT**...

REALLY?

GUESS WHAT IT IS!

SHAKE!

SHAKE!

SHAKE!

ANY IDEA?

NOT A CLUE!

RATTLE! RATTLE!

OPEN THAT SUCKER!!

IN RETROSPECT, A **BEEHIVE** MAY NOT HAVE BEEN THE BEST GIFT...

I **HATE** BIRTHDAYS.

MORNING, ROY! I GOT YOU A **LATTE**!
YOU KNOW I'M **LACTOSE INTOLERANT**.
JOHNSON

IT'S MADE WITH **SOY**.
PRETTY SMALL CUP.

IT'S THE **LARGEST** THEY MAKE.
HMMPH... FINE. I GUESS I'LL **CHOKE** IT DOWN.

PRE-CAFFEINE ROY IS MY **LEAST** FAVORITE ROY OF ALL.
NO WHIPPED CREAM?!? NEXT TIME JUST HAVE THEM @#$☆ IN THE CUP!

YOU KNOW, ROY OL BOY, THIS IS THE **LIFE**.
IT SURE IS.

I DON T THINK I VE **EVER** BEEN MORE RELAXED.
ME EITHER.
JOHNSON

BLOOP!
BLOOP!
BLOOP!

THAT S A LITTLE **TOO RELAXED**.
IT WAS THE TRUNKS!!!

YOU SURE YOU SAW THE **WATER SNAKE** OVER HERE?
I THINK SO.
JOHNSON

KEEP AN EYE OUT... I **STILL** DON T SEE IT.

THE THINGS ARE SO **SMALL**... WE PROBABLY WENT RIGHT PAST IT.

POOR THING IS PROBABLY SCARED TO DEATH OF US.

ROY, FOR THE **LAST TIME**, I'M **SORRY**!
JOHNSON

I HAD **NO IDEA** THAT SNAKE WAS WRAPPED AROUND YOU...

WILL YOU QUIT BEING A **BABY** AND COME OUT OF THERE?

BERNIE, DO YOU HAVE ANY IDEA HOW **PAINFUL** THIS IS?
YOU LOOK LIKE AN ANGRY Q-TIP.

YOU BEEN EATING **HUNTERS**, BENTLEY?
WHY WOULD YOU ASK THAT, ROY? YOU KNOW I QUIT.
JOHNSON

BECAUSE YOU RE WEARING A **HUNTER S CAP** AND POLKA DOT **UNDERPANTS**.
HHMMPPHH!

BLLAAARRRGGHHH!!!!!

AND YOU JUST BARFED UP A HUNTING RIFLE.
I NEEDED A TOOTHPICK.

HEY, OZ, HOW'S IT GOING.
ANOTHER DAY IN THE PARK, DONOVAN.

SAY... DO I HAVE SOMETHING STUCK IN MY TAIL?
LOOKS LIKE GUM.
JOHNSON

OH THIS IS JUST **GREAT**... COULD MY LIFE GET ANY WORSE?
YOU COULD LIVE ON A **BENCH** IN A **PARK**.

YOU SURE KNOW HOW TO PUT THINGS INTO PERSPECTIVE, OZ.
STEP INTO MY KITCHEN AND WE'LL SEE ABOUT GETTING THAT GUM OUT.

The untitled "Project Park" only lasted 6 strips as well. This was exactly how long it took me to realize that a homeless man on a bench doesn't really make for many comedic moments.

HOW LONG HAVE WE KNOWN EACH OTHER, OZ?
OH... BOUT TWO YEARS NOW.
JOHNSON

TWO YEARS, MAN... AND I DON'T EVEN FEEL LIKE I **KNOW** YOU.
WHAT'S TO KNOW?

HOW'D YOU GET HERE? WHY'D YOU STAY? WHERE ARE YOU GOING?
LONG STORY, LONGER STORY, TO GET A HOTDOG.

THANKS A **HEAP** FOR OPENING UP, OZ.
COME ON... I'LL BUY YOU A KETCHUP PACKET.

MORNING, VIN!
I GOT **NO** FREE DOGS TODAY, OZ.
HOT DOGS YUM! $2.00
JOHNSON

VIN DOESN'T HAVE **ANY** FREE HOTDOGS TODAY, OZ.
THAT'S A **REAL** SHAME, DONVAN.
HEY... JUST WHAT **EXACTLY** IS YOU TWO DRIVING AT?

OH MY LORD!!! LOOK AT THE SIZE OF THAT RAT!!!
BOO!
FINE!!! TAKE YOUR **STINKIN'** HOTDOG!
HOT DOGS YUM! $2.00

YOU KNOW, DONOVAN, LIFE IS LIKE A HOTDOG.

SOME HAVE TO HAVE ALL OF THIS **STUFF** ON THEIR DOG, LIKE RELISH, KETCHUP AND ONIONS. JUST LIKE SOME HAVE TO HAVE NICE CARS, CLOTHES AND HOMES.

THEN THERE ARE THOSE OF US WHO ARE JUST FINE EATING OUR HOTDOGS PLAIN. **RIGHT, BUDDY**?
JOHNSON

IS THIS A BAD TIME TO ASK YOU TO GO GRAB ME SOME RELISH?

JOHNSON
SPLOIT!
FOOOM!

SKREEEEEEEE

LIKE I WAS SAYING...
BUTTON IT, FUZZ FACE!!!

MORNING, OZ.
WHATEVER.

SOMEONE GET UP ON THE WRONG SIDE OF THE BENCH THIS MORNING?
OH, HA HA.

HEY CHILL OUT, MAN, IT'S THANKSGIVING... A TIME FOR LOVED ONES AND... OH...
YEAH.

SORRY... I FORGET SOMETIMES.
STUPID HOLIDAY.
JOHNSON

JOCK

GUEST STRIPS

One of the most amazing parts about drawing this comic strip was that I was fortunate enough to be surrounded by some amazing artists and writers who had their own strips.

So I did what anyone in my position would do... I asked them to draw my comic for me every chance I got.

Thanks to every single artist who took the time to draw my dumb characters!

...I SHOULD HAVE BOUGHT A HAMSTER.
CUT! THAT'S A WRAP!
HOW WAS THAT? TOO MUCH? IT FELT KIND OF FORCED...
DUDE. IT'S A WEB COMIC.
HEY DALE!
YO!
FREAKIN' GUY THINKS IT'S FREAKIN' SHAKESPEARE FOR CRYIN' OUT LOUD...
DALE, WE NEED TO TALK.
SURE THING, DYLAN. WHAT'S UP?
DALE, MY NAME IS DANNY.
OF COURSE IT IS.

LOOK... THE READER POLL RESULTS JUST CAME IN... IT LOOKS LIKE WE'RE TAKING YOUR CHARACTER IN A NEW DIRECTION.
OH GREAT, NOT ANOTHER NOSE JOB...
NO, IT'S WORSE. SEE, THE READERS FEEL THAT YOU SHOULD HAVE A MORE ACTIVE LOVE LIFE. SO WE'RE SETTING YOU UP ON A BLIND DATE...
HOW COULD A LITTLE DATE BE WORSE THAN PAINFUL RECONSTRUCTIVE SURGERY?
OH.. YOU'LL SEE.
LATER...
SO... WHERE ARE YOU FROM... ORIGINALLY?
HMPH.

SLAM!

SID, ANGUS, SLOW DOWN! WHERE'S THE FIRE?

BOOM
FOOM

DAN THOMPSON
DOES THAT ANSWER YOUR QUESTION, DALE?
C-4 IS NOT A TOY!

ANGUS! CAN'T YOU PICK UP SOME OF YOUR TRASH!
THE STORE LOOKS LIKE A DUMP, AND I CAN'T MAKE ANY SALES LIKE THIS!
IT'S NOT MY FAULT. I'M HYPOGLYCEMIC.

WHAT'S THIS?
LOOKS LIKE THE MAIL IS HERE...
NOW WHY IS DALE GETTING MAIL FROM THE AMERICAN MEDICAL RESEARCH CENTER?

"DEAR SIR,
THANK YOU FOR REQUESTING INFORMATION REGARDING THE DONATION OF GERBILS FOR INVASIVE MEDICAL TESTING. WE ARE CURRENTLY PAYING HANDSOMELY FOR GERBILS. ESPECIALLY GERBILS WITH A HISTORY OF OVEREATING."
GYAAAGH!!!!
HEY, DALE!
LOOK AT ME EARNING MY KEEP, MAKIN' THE STORE ALL PRETTY!
I SURE AM GREAT TO KEEP AROUND, AIN'T I?
"AMERICAN MEDICAL RESEARCH CENTER"?
I MADE IT UP. IT KEEPS HIM ON HIS TOES.

IMAGINE WHAT OUR STRIPS WOULD BE LIKE IF WE WALKED THE WAY OUR REAL LIFE COUNTERPARTS WALK...

I FEEL DIRTY, BOB...
...ME TOO SID...
ALA DAVE JOHNSON

IF I CAN'T HAVE A GERBIL, CAN I AT LEAST HAVE A DOG??
DOGS ARE WORSE...

HOW ABOUT A MONKEY, THEN?
MONKEYS ARE THE FILTHIEST OF ALL. HAVE YOU EVER TRIED TO BATHE A MONKEY? NO ONE HAS.
MEL HENZE

DO YOU SEE WHAT I'M GETTING AT HERE, GUYS?
I TOLD YOU, IT'S A GLANDULAR PROBLEM...
I LIKE LOTS OF BUBBLES, FLOATING CANDLES AND JIM CROCE MUSIC.

HEY SID, CHECK THIS OUT!
WHEN I GET CLOSER TO THE RADIO THE SIGNAL COMES IN BETTER.

WHEN I BACK UP, IT GOES OUT AGAIN!
ISN'T THAT COOL?
TWIDDLE TWIDDLE
TWIDDLE TWIDDLE

SID?
POIT!

HEY LOOK! GOLF-CARTS FOR SALE!
WHO DO WE KNOW THAT WOULD LOVE ONE OF THESE AND IS WELL PASSED DRIVING AGE...IN UH... DOG YEARS...?
TWIDDLE TWIDDLE
TWIDDLE

No, mom, everything is fine here... really...

Dale! The blender exploded, the couch is on fire, and Bob's aliens are living in our bathtub!

What? No, no... that was just the television...
Tom T

You ever wonder if your soulmate is somewhere out there, Baxter
Not really.

Not really?! What if She's out there waiting for you right now and you're not even thinking about her?!

Well, if she's my soulmate she's probably the patient type.
She's also probably very stupid.

DAVE JOHNSON'S *DOG COMPLEX*

HEY, *SID*. THIS IS *PUMPKIN*.
SHE HELPS DOGS UNDERSTAND THE JOY'S OF *BEING* A DOG.
UH... *HEY!*
NOW *SID*... IS A *HANDSHAKE* HOW DOGS SAY *HELLO?*

THIS IS HOW DOGS INTRODUCE EACH OTHER.
SNIFF SNIFF

HEY, LADY!! KEEP IT TO *YOURSELF!!*
COME NOW, SID... YOU NEED TO GET IN *TOUCH* WITH YOUR INNER PUPPY!

HEY, BAX... THIS DOG'S *NUTS!*
SHE WANT'S ME TO *"TOUCH"* PUPPIES!
AHHH... A *CHALLENGE!*

HI JOE
HI FRANK

GEORGE, ARE YOU FEELING ALL RIGHT ?
YOU LOOK FUNNY
NOW THAT I THINK ABOUT IT I DO FEEL FUNNY

MAYBE YOU GOT TOO MUCH SUN OR SOMETHING
YEAH

OR YOU'VE GOT A DOG COMPLEX

DAN THOMPSON

DALE, I HAVE TO ASK YOU A SERIOUS **QUESTION**...

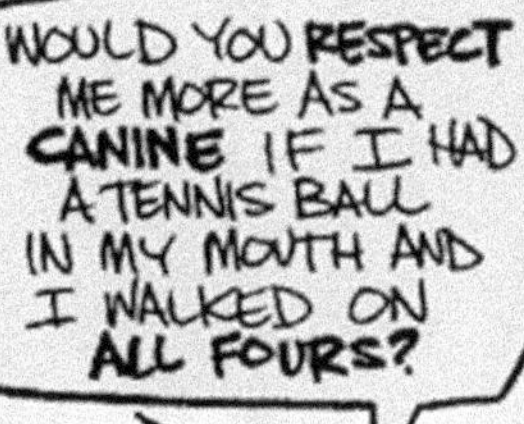
WOULD YOU **RESPECT** ME MORE AS A **CANINE** IF I HAD A TENNIS BALL IN MY MOUTH AND I WALKED ON **ALL FOURS?**

THAT'S IT— NO MORE **DR. PHIL**...

Now I *love* Law and Order but why does Lenny Brisco have to go through as many partners as he does?
Well think about it...

I mean it makes sense for a show like *Law & Order* to keep their options open.
After all that kind of variety is what keeps long running shows like that from getting stale.

Wow, I never *thought* of it that way...
I have. Trust me

WHAT DID YOU BRING ME?!!
WHERE'S MY NEWSPAPER? MY SLIPPERS?

MOST DOGS BRING SOMETHING TO THEIR MASTER. YOU? NOTHING.
I DO PLENTY! YA KNOW, IF WE ARE GOING TO CONTINUE LIVING TOGETHER YOU'RE GONNA HAVE TO GIVE ME A LITTLE CREDIT.

YOU'RE RIGHT. I'M SORRY. IT'S BEEN A LONG DAY.
YA-YA, NOW PASS ME MY NEWSPAPER.

HELLO. YOU MIGHT RECOGNIZE ME AS "BOB" FROM THE HIT WEBCOMIC ***DEAD AIR***. YOU KNOW, IN ***DEAD AIR*** I PLAY A PRETTY WACKY CHARACTER. BUT IN REAL LIFE, I'M JUST A REGULAR NORMAL GUY.

SO REMEMBER, THE NEXT TIME YOU PASS A JANITOR OR MAINTENANCE MAN IN ***YOUR*** BUILDING, ***REMEMBER:*** HE'S JUST A NORMAL GUY LIKE YOU. AND THERE'S NOTHING TO BE SUSPICIOUS ABOUT.

...ESPECIALLY THE ***BOILER ROOM***. BECAUSE THERE'S NOTHING IN THERE. NOT A THING. NOPE. NO NEED TO GO IN THERE TO SEE WHAT THOSE NOISES WERE.

...ALSO REMEMBER TO WRAP YOUR HEAD IN ***TIN FOIL*** EVERY DAY, TO PREVENT THE SHADOW GOVERNMENT FROM POLICING YOUR THOUGHTS.
I'M NOT WEARING ANY PANTS!
More you Know

ALRITE, SID!
WHY WERE EIGHT CHEESE PIZZAS JUST DELIVERED TO OUR DOOR?

WHAT?! HOW COULD I HAVE DONE IT? I'M JUST A DOG!

I MEAN UH...ARF
NOW WHERE'D YOU PUT THOSE PIZZAS?

DANNY, DID YOU SCREEN OUR CALLS, I'D LIKE TO GET SOME INTERESTING ONES FOR ONCE
OFF AIR

SURE DID, DALE.

OKAY, WE'RE BACK, FOLKS, AND WITH A CALLER. GO AHEAD, CALLER.
YEAH, HI. I JUST WANTED TO KNOW HOW A LOSER LIKE YOU GOT ON THE RADIO.
ON AIR

WHAT? I WAS WONDERING THAT MYSELF.

How was work, Dale?
Not so good, Danny really messed up.

Did you eat him?
No, why would I do that?

That's what animals do, eat the weak.
Well, humans don't

Oh right, you probably test for diseases first.
Bingo, you got it, sid.

SO I WAS THINKING MAYBE LATER WE'D GO OVER TO THE PARK AND...
NO CAN DO, DALE. I'M TAKING A ME DAY.

...A ME DAY?
OH YEAH. NOTHING BUT BON BONS AND BUBBLE BATHS FOR ME, MY FRIEND.

...AND JUST WHAT, PRAY TELL, IS ALL OVER YOUR FACE?
OH, JUST BECAUSE I'M A DOG I CAN'T EXFOLIATE?

...YOU'VE BEEN READING OPRAH MAGAZINE AGAIN, HAVEN'T YOU?
FAT-FREE LEMON SQUARE?

Concept Art, Extras, and Other Junk

SO, I SAID TO HER, LISTEN, LADY, I THINK I KNOW A THING OR TWO ABOUT FIREWORK SAFETY. NOW ARE YOU GOING TO SELL ME THE CRAP OR NOT?

BIG BLAST

HAPPY 4TH OF JULY!!!

FROM: THE GANG AT DOG COMPLEX

HAVE YOU HEARD ABOUT THAT GUY WHO'S BEEN KILLING ALL THE *NUTS* AROUND TOWN?
NO! ARE YOU SERIOUS?

YEP. THEY RELEASED A *PHOTO* OF HIM.
DRAWED BY JOHNSON, FOR PAGE, WITH TONS OF ADMIRATION

HA! HA! HA! HA! HA! HA! HA!
SEE, THAT AIN'T EVEN FUNNY, MAN.
JOHNSON

Guest strip drawn for Frank Page's "Bob the Squirrel."

ROCK IT LIKE YOU'VE GOT A MULLET

HEY, BUG, MY COUSIN'S HERE FOR A VISIT!
OH MAN... HE'S ALWAYS WANTING TO BORROW MY PHONE.
LUCKY CHARMS

PHONE HOME?
SEE!

OKAY, THIS IS JUST LAME.
WHAT?
PHONE?
LUCKY CHARMS

WE'RE MAKING E.T. JOKES. WHAT'S NEXT? ALF?!?
WE DO THAT AND I'M QUITTING.
LUCKY CHARMS

Guest strip for Tim Andress' "Bug and Slug" comic.

MAKE-UP
HAIRBALLS
ANXIETY SUCKS
DANDELION SEED
EXTRA BILL DROOL
SOMETHING TELLS ME I'M ON THE WRONG SET AGAIN.

Guest strip for David Wright for his comic, "Todd and Penguin." Apologies to Mr. Breathed.

DEAD AIR PRESENTS:

SMOKEY AND THE DIMWIT

DALE FLEMING AS "THE BANDIT"

SID AS "FROG"

DANNY AS "SNOWMAN"

THIS PLANET IS SO *BORING* SOMETIMES!
WE COULD PLAY CHECKERS.

NO, NO, I NEED MORE THAN CHECKERS TODAY. I WANT TO REALLY *LIVE*!
HOW SO?

I WANT TO DO SOMETHING I HAVE *NO BUSINESS* DOING. SOMETHING I'M NOT EVEN *QUALIFIED* FOR AND JUST *WING IT!*
I DON'T LIKE WHERE THIS IS GOING.

CNN NEWS WHEN YOU DON'T WANT IT!
8:03 AM EST
TOP STORY
DEN - 78 PARTLY SUNNY
LATEST CANDIDATE THROWS HAT IN RING FOR CALIFORNIA GOV
MAN ANGERED THAT BLUE MOON NOT SYNDICAT

Guest strip for Terry Person, for his comic, "Blue Moon."

THE TECHNO GEEK
WITH TECHNOLOGY COMES A SURPRISING AMOUNT OF CHAFING.
NIGHT VISION DEVICE
MP3 PLAYER WITH 100% LEGAL EDDIE MONEY SONGS
POWER SUPPLY AND OPTIONAL FORMAN GRILL
WATCH AND GPS TRACKING DEVICE
LAPTOP COMPUTER WITH OPTIONAL TOASTER. BURN MORE THAN JUST YOUR CDS!
ELECTRIC PANTS
DOG COMPLEX

REAL MEN DON'T WEAR PANTS.

DO YA' THINK?
I THINK YOU MAY HAVE USED A BIT TOO MUCH LIGHTER FLUID.

DOG COMPLEX
JOHNSON

WILLY
THE
PARROT
DOG
COMPLEX
WWW.DOG-COMPLEX.COM
A.C.
THE ALLEY
CAT
DOG
COMPLEX
WWW.DOG-COMPLEX.COM
ANGUS
THE GERBIL
DOG
COMPLEX
WWW.DOG-COMPLEX.COM
CHASE
THE
LIZARD
DOG
COMPLEX
WWW.DOG-COMPLEX.COM

UNCLE SID'S PIZZA SHACK

Home of the world famous dog treat pizza!

"Steaming hot pie, that's fit for a dog!"

At one point, I decided that I was going to make a comic book style adventure involving the gang. These next two pages are the only ones I ever drew for it. Very short comic book.

THE FLIGHT...
THERE S A CHICKEN ON MY LAP...
AT LEAST WE GET TO SEE GILI !
AM I THE ONLY ONE WHO S CHAFFING?
THE NATIVES...
I WAS JUST ASKING FOR A STARBUCKS!!!
OUR ELEPHANT SMELLS LIKE WET FOOT.
THE ELEPHANTS...
HEY, SID! LET S TAKE A SHORT-CUT THROUGH THAT SWAMP!!!
FOR THE LAST TIME, I M SORRY!!!
THE LEECHES...
EXACTLY HOW BIG IS HUGE?
THE INSECTS...
ALL LEADING TO THE REMOTE, MOUNTAIN-TOP VILLAGE...

IS THIS REFERRING THING SAFE? IT SURE DOESN'T SOUND SAFE.

OKAY, NAME IS SID... UH... DOG. EMAIL IS SID@DOG-COMPLEX.COM. PASSWORD... LET'S SEE... HOW ABOUT MUFFINBUTT1.

I WROTE MINE DOWN ON MY SANDWICH!

NO, YOU HEARD ME CORRECTLY... I WANT YOU TO SHAVE THE URL ON THIS SANDWICH INTO MY BACK.

WOW! LOOK AT ALL THIS GREAT STUFF! THANKS DOG COMPLEX!!

JOHN TESH PHOTO

SHOE

HALF EATEN DING DONG

TOMATO SOUP CAN

MISSHAPEN BOWLING BALL

This series of drawings was for a referral program I came up with to drive new folks to the strip. The amazing Peter Crouch at rivergum.net coded the whole thing, and it worked like a champ!

THIS ARTICLE SAYS THAT THERE IS A **SURGERY** YOU CAN HAVE PERFORMED ON YOUR DOG TO REMOVE ITS **BARK**, SO IT CAN'T MAKE **A SOUND**.

12/03/04

JOHNSON

AM I **REALLY** THAT ANNOYING?
JUST MAKING CONVERSATION.

There you have it. I may not have made you love "Dog Complex," but I hope I at least got a chuckle or two out of you. Keep checking www.3Dave.com from time to time, as you never know when Sid and the gang might drop by for a visit. Thanks for reading!

THE END

www.ingramcontent.com/pod-product-compliance
Ingram Content Group UK Ltd.
Pitfield, Milton Keynes, MK11 3LW, UK
UKHW051138260726
13967UKWH00010B/3115